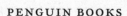

PENGUIN BOOKS

A BEAUTIFUL DAY *in the* NEIGHBORHOOD

Fred Rogers (1928–2003) was a producer, writer, magician, puppeteer, minister, husband, and father who began working in children's television in the 1950s and created the PBS program *Mister Rogers' Neighborhood*. He pioneered "programming that spoke, with respect, to the concerns of early childhood, not as adults see it but as children feel it." For his work, he received the Presidential Medal of Freedom, a Peabody Award, and numerous other honors. The Television Hall of Fame inducted him in 1999, and the Smithsonian Institution displays one of his sweaters as a "treasure of American history." He founded Family Communications, Inc., now Fred Rogers Productions, a not-for-profit company that continues to develop programming, special projects, and materials that help children learn and grow, including *Daniel Tiger's Neighborhood*.

Tom Junod is the recipient of two National Magazine Awards from the American Society of Magazine Editors. He has written for *GQ* and *Esquire*, and is a senior writer for ESPN. His 1998 profile of Fred Rogers for *Esquire* is the basis for the feature film *A Beautiful Day in the Neighborhood*.

ALSO BY FRED ROGERS

Dear Mister Rogers, Does It Ever Rain in Your Neighborhood?: Letters to Mister Rogers

A

BEAUTIFUL DAY

in the

NEIGHBORHOOD

Neighborly Words of Wisdom
from Mister Rogers

FRED ROGERS

Including the essay by Tom Junod
that inspired the major motion picture

• Previously published as *You Are Special* •

PENGUIN BOOKS

PENGUIN BOOKS
An imprint of Penguin Random House LLC
penguinrandomhouse.com

First published in the United States of America as *You Are Special: Words of Wisdom for All
Ages from a Beloved Neighbor* by Viking, an imprint of Penguin Publishing Group,
a division of Penguin Random House LLC, 1994
Published in Penguin Books 1995
This edition entitled *A Beautiful Day in the Neighborhood* published in Penguin Books 2019

Portions of this work first appeared in Fred Rogers's books,
How Families Grow, Mister Rogers' Playbook, and *Mister Rogers Talks with Parents*,
and his column "Insights into Childhood" (King Features Syndicate).

"Can You Say . . . Hero?" by Tom Junod first appeared in the November 1998 issue of *Esquire*.

The song lyrics in this volume are reprinted from the following compositions: "I Like to Be
Told," © 1970, Fred M. Rogers; "I Need You," © 1970, Fred M. Rogers; "I'm Taking Care of You,"
© 1968, Fred M. Rogers; "It's the People You Like the Most," © 1972, Fred M. Rogers; "It's You I
Like," © 1960, Fred M. Rogers; "Please Don't Think It's Funny," © 1968, Fred M. Rogers;
"Pretending," © 1971, Fred M. Rogers; "Sometimes People Are Good," © 1967, Fred M. Rogers;
"The Truth Will Make Me Free," © 1970, Fred M. Rogers; "You're Growing," 1967, Fred M.
Rogers; "You've Got to Do It," © 1969, Fred M. Rogers.

Grateful acknowledgment is made for permission to reprint an excerpt from
"Whatever Happened to Old Fashioned Love" by Lewis Anderson. © 1981 Careers-
BMG Music Publishing, Inc. (BMI). All rights reserved. Used by permission.

LIBRARY OF CONGRESS CATALOGING-IN-PUBLICATION DATA
Names: Rogers, Fred, author. | Junod, Tom, author.
Title: A beautiful day in the neighborhood : neighborly words of wisdom from Mister Rogers /
Fred Rogers ; including the essay by Tom Junod that inspired the major motion picture.
Other titles: You are special
Description: New York : Penguin Books, 2019. | Originally published: New York,
N.Y.: Viking, 1994, under title, You are special.
Identifiers: LCCN 2019027644 (print) | LCCN 2019027645 (ebook) |
ISBN 9780143135388 (paperback) | ISBN 9780525507055 (ebook)
Subjects: LCSH: Self-esteem. | Child rearing.
Classification: LCC BF697.5.S46 R64 2019 (print) | LCC BF697.5.S46 (ebook) | DDC 158.1—dc23
LC record available at https://lccn.loc.gov/2019027644
LC ebook record available at https://lccn.loc.gov/2019027645

Printed in the United States of America
1 3 5 7 9 10 8 6 4 2

Set in Minion Pro • Designed by Sabrina Bowers

*Dedicated to all of the children—of any age—
who have found our "Neighborhood" and have been
willing to spend time growing right along with me.*

Contents

Can You Say . . . Hero?

Tom Junod

In 1998, journalist Tom Junod received an assignment to profile Fred Rogers for Esquire. *For reasons both personal and professional, Junod had lost confidence as a writer. He didn't anticipate finding guidance and reassurance from such an unlikely source, a beloved children's television host. In crafting the piece, Junod followed Rogers around New York City, visiting his apartment and studio to observe his daily routines and interactions with adoring fans. He also accompanied Rogers to the home where he grew up in Latrobe, Pennsylvania, for a window into the childhood of a man renowned for his understanding of children. The resulting piece, which beautifully demonstrated why Fred Rogers means so much to so many people, was widely acclaimed on publication and became known as a classic of magazine reporting.*

When screenwriters Noah Harpster and Micah Fitzerman-Blue read Junod's piece, they were inspired to write a story based on the true-life friendship between the two men. Directed by Marielle Heller and starring two-time Oscar-winner Tom Hanks as Fred Rogers and Matthew Rhys as Lloyd Vogel, a character based on Junod, the film is called A Beautiful Day in the Neighborhood, *released in 2019 by TriStar Pictures. "This friendship between these two men was an irresistible opportunity to revisit the philosophy of Fred Rogers through a grown-up lens," said Marielle Heller. "At a time when the world feels divided,*

Fred's message of kindness is even more important. His radical kindness, one that does not discriminate, resonated with all of us and we hope it resonates with audiences. We all feel like we've been forever changed by working on this movie and we thank Fred for that gift."

ONCE UPON A TIME, a little boy loved a stuffed animal whose name was Old Rabbit. It was so old, in fact, that it was really an unstuffed animal; so old that even back then, with the little boy's brain still nice and fresh, he had no memory of it as "Young Rabbit," or even "Rabbit"; so old that Old Rabbit was barely a rabbit at all but rather a greasy hunk of skin without eyes and ears, with a single red stitch where its tongue used to be. The little boy didn't know why he loved Old Rabbit; he just did, and the night he threw it out the car window was the night he learned how to pray. He would grow up to become a great prayer, this little boy, but only intermittently, only fitfully, praying only when fear and desperation drove him to it, and the night he threw Old Rabbit into the darkness was the night that set the pattern, the night that taught him how. He prayed for Old Rabbit's safe return, and when, hours later, his mother and father came home with the filthy, precious strip of rabbity roadkill, he learned not only that prayers are sometimes answered but also the kind of severe effort they entail, the kind of endless frantic summoning. And so when he threw Old Rabbit out the car window the *next time*, it was gone for good.

You were a child once, too. That's what Mister Rogers said, that's what he wrote down, once upon a time, for the doctors. The doctors were ophthalmologists. An ophthalmologist is a doctor who takes care of the eyes. Sometimes, ophthalmologists have to take care of the eyes of children, and some children get very scared, because children know that their world disappears when their eyes close, and they can be afraid that the ophthalmologists will make their eyes close forever. The ophthalmologists did not want to scare children, so they asked Mister Rogers for help, and Mister Rogers agreed to write a chapter for a book the ophthalmologists were putting together—a chapter about what other ophthalmologists could do to calm the children who came to their offices. Because Mister Rogers is such a busy man, however, he could not write the chapter himself, and he asked a woman who worked for him to write it instead. She worked very hard at writing the chapter, until one day she showed what she had written to Mister Rogers, who read it and crossed it all out and wrote a sentence addressed directly to the doctors who would be reading it: "You were a child once, too."

And that's how the chapter began.

The old navy-blue sport jacket comes off first, then the dress shoes, except that now there is not the famous sweater or the famous sneakers to replace them, and so after the shoes he's on to the dark socks, peeling them off and showing the blanched skin of his narrow feet. The tie is next, the scanty black batwing of a bow tie hand-tied at his slender throat, and then the shirt, always white or light blue, whisked from his body button by button. He wears an undershirt, of course, but no matter—soon that's gone, too, as is the belt, as are the beige trousers, until his undershorts stand as the last impediment to his nakedness. They are boxers, egg-colored, and to rid himself of them he bends at the waist, and stands on one leg, and hops, and lifts one knee toward his chest and then the other and then . . . Mister Rogers has no clothes on.

Nearly every morning of his life, Mister Rogers has gone swimming, and now, here he is, standing in a locker room, seventy years old and as white as the Easter Bunny, rimed with frost wherever he has hair, gnawed pink in the spots where his dry skin has gone to flaking, slightly wattled at the neck, slightly stooped at the shoulder, slightly sunken in the chest, slightly curvy at the hips, slightly pigeoned at the toes, slightly aswing at the fine bobbing nest of himself . . . and yet when he speaks, it is in that voice, his voice, the famous one, the unmistakable one, the televised one, the voice dressed in sweater and sneakers, the soft one, the reassuring one, the curious and expository one, the sly voice that sounds adult to the ears of children and childish to the ears of adults, and what he says, in the midst of all his bobbing nudity, is as under-stated as it is obvious: "Well, Tom, I guess you've already gotten a deeper glimpse into my daily routine than most people have."

Once upon a time, a long time ago, a man took off his jacket and put on a sweater. Then he took off his shoes and put on a pair of sneakers. His name was Fred Rogers. He was starting a television program, aimed at children, called *Mister Rogers' Neighborhood.* He had been on television before, but only as the voices and move-ments of puppets, on a program called *The Children's Corner.* Now he was stepping in front of the camera as Mister Rogers, and he wanted to do things right, and whatever he did right, he wanted to repeat. And so, once upon a time, Fred Rogers took off his jacket and put on a sweater his mother had made him, a cardigan with a zipper. Then he took off his shoes and put on a pair of navy-blue canvas boating sneakers. He did the same thing the next day, and then the next . . . until he had done the same things, those things, 865 times, at the beginning of 865 television programs, over a span of thirty-one years. The first time I met Mister Rogers, he told me a story of how deeply his simple gestures had been felt, and received. He had just come back from visiting Koko, the gorilla who has learned—or who has been taught—American Sign Language. Koko watches television. Koko watches *Mister Rogers' Neighborhood*, and when Mister Rogers, in his sweater and sneakers, entered the place where she lives, Koko immediately folded him in her long, black arms, as though he were a child, and then . . . "She took my shoes off, Tom," Mister Rogers said.

Koko was much bigger than Mister Rogers. She weighed 280 pounds, and Mister Rogers weighed 143. Koko weighed 280 pounds because she is a gorilla, and Mister Rogers weighed 143 pounds because he has weighed 143 pounds as long as he has been Mister Rogers, because once upon a time, around thirty-one years ago, Mister Rogers stepped on a scale, and the scale told him that Mister Rogers weighs 143 pounds. No, not that he *weighed* 143 pounds, but that he *weighs* 143 pounds. . . . And so, every day, Mister Rogers refuses to do anything that would make his weight change—he neither drinks, nor smokes, nor eats flesh of any kind, nor goes to bed late at night, nor sleeps late in the morning, nor even watches television—and every morning, when he swims, he steps on a scale in his bathing suit and his bathing cap and his goggles, and the scale tells him that he weighs 143 pounds. This has happened so many times that Mister Rogers has come to see that number as a gift, as a destiny fulfilled, because, as he says, "the number 143 means 'I love you.' It takes one letter to say 'I' and four letters to say 'love' and three letters to say 'you.' One hundred and forty-three. 'I love you.' Isn't that wonderful?"

The first time I called Mister Rogers on the telephone, I woke him up from his nap. He takes a nap every day in the late afternoon— just as he wakes up every morning at five-thirty to read and study and write and pray for the legions who have requested his prayers; just as he goes to bed at nine-thirty at night and sleeps eight hours without interruption. On this afternoon, the end of a hot, yellow day in New York City, he was very tired, and when I asked if I could go to his apartment and see him, he paused for a moment and said shyly, "Well, Tom, I'm in my bathrobe, if you don't mind." I told him I didn't mind, and when, five minutes later, I took the elevator to his floor, well, sure enough, there was Mister Rogers, silver-haired, standing in the golden door at the end of the hallway and wearing eyeglasses and suede moccasins with rawhide laces and a flimsy old blue-and-yellow bathrobe that revealed whatever part of his skinny white calves his dark-blue dress socks didn't hide. "Welcome, Tom," he said with a slight bow, and bade me follow him inside, where he lay down—no, *stretched out*, as though he had known me all his life—on a couch upholstered with gold velveteen. He rested his head on a small pillow and kept his eyes closed while he explained that he had bought the apartment thirty years before for $11,000 and kept it for whenever he came to New York on business for the Neighborhood. I sat in an old armchair and looked around. The place was drab and dim, with the smell of stalled air and a stain of daguerreotype sunlight on its closed, slatted blinds, and Mister Rogers looked so at home in its gloomy familiarity that I thought he was going to fall back asleep when suddenly the phone rang, startling him. "Oh, hello, my dear," he said when he picked it up, and then he said that he had a visitor, someone who wanted to learn more about the Neighborhood. "Would you like to speak to him?" he asked, and then handed me the phone. "It's Joanne," he said. I took the phone and spoke to a woman—his wife, the mother of his two sons—whose voice was hearty and almost whooping in its forthrightness and who spoke to me as though she had known me for a long time and was making the effort to keep up the acquaintance. When I handed him back the phone, he said, "Bye, my dear," and hung up and curled on the couch like a cat, with his bare calves swirled underneath him and one of his hands gripping his ankle, so that he looked as languorous as an odalisque. There was an energy to him, however, a fearlessness, an unashamed insistence on intimacy, and though I tried to ask him questions about himself, he always turned the questions back on me, and when I finally got him to talk about the puppets that were the comfort of his lonely boyhood, he looked at me, his gray-blue eyes at once mild and steady, and asked,

"What about you, Tom? Did you have any special friends growing up?"

"Special friends?"

"Yes," he said.

"Maybe a puppet, or a special toy, or maybe just a stuffed animal you loved very much. Did you have a special friend like that, Tom?"

"Yes, Mister Rogers."

"Did your special friend have a name, Tom?"

"Yes, Mister Rogers. His name was Old Rabbit."

"Old Rabbit. Oh, and I'll bet the two of you were together since he was a very young rabbit. Would you like to tell me about Old Rabbit, Tom?"

And it was just about then, when I was spilling the beans about my special friend, that Mister Rogers rose from his corner of the couch and stood suddenly in front of me with a small black camera in hand. "Can I take your picture, Tom?" he asked. "I'd like to take your picture. I like to take pictures of all my new friends, so that I can show them to Joanne. . . ." And then, in the dark room, there was a wallop of white light, and Mister Rogers disappeared behind it.

Once upon a time, there was a boy who didn't like himself very much. It was not his fault. He was born with cerebral palsy. Cerebral palsy is something that happens to the brain. It means that you can think but sometimes can't walk, or even talk. This boy had a very bad case of cerebral palsy, and when he was still a little boy, some of the people entrusted to take care of him took advantage of him instead and did things to him that made him think that he was a very bad little boy, because only a bad little boy would have to live with the things he had to live with. In fact, when the little boy grew up to be a teenager, he would get so mad at himself that he would hit himself, hard, with his own fists and tell his mother, on the computer he used for a mouth, that he didn't want to live anymore, for he was sure that God didn't like what was inside him any more than he did. He had always loved Mister Rogers, though, and now, even when he was fourteen years old, he watched the Neighborhood whenever it was on, and the boy's mother sometimes thought that Mister Rogers was keeping her son alive. She and the boy lived together in a city in California, and although she wanted very much for her son to meet Mister Rogers, she knew that he was far too disabled to travel all the way to Pittsburgh, so she figured he would never meet his hero, until one day she learned through a special foundation designed to help children like her son that Mister Rogers was coming to California and that after he visited the gorilla named Koko, he was coming to meet her son.

At first, the boy was made very nervous by the thought that Mister Rogers was visiting him. He was so nervous, in fact, that when Mister Rogers did visit, he got mad at himself and began hating himself and hitting himself, and his mother had to take him to another room and talk to him. Mister Rogers didn't leave, though. He wanted something from the boy, and Mister Rogers never leaves when he wants something from somebody. He just waited patiently, and when the boy came back, Mister Rogers talked to him, and then he made his request. He said, "I would like you to do something for me. Would you do something for me?" On his computer, the boy answered yes, of course, he would do *anything* for Mister Rogers, so then Mister Rogers said, "I would like you to pray for me. Will you pray for me?" And now the boy didn't know how to respond. He was thunderstruck. Thunderstruck means that you can't talk, because something has happened that's as sudden and as miraculous and maybe as scary as a bolt of lightning, and all you can do is listen to the rumble. The boy was thunderstruck because nobody had ever *asked* him for something like that, ever. The boy had always been prayed *for*. The boy had always been the *object* of prayer, and now he was being asked to pray for Mister Rogers, and although at first he didn't know if he could do it, he said he would, he said he'd try, and ever since then he keeps Mister Rogers in his prayers and doesn't talk about wanting to die anymore, because he figures Mister Rogers is close to God, and if Mister Rogers likes him, that must mean God likes him, too.

As for Mister Rogers himself . . . well, he doesn't look at the story in the same way that the boy did or that I did. In fact, when Mister Rogers first told me the story, I complimented him on being so smart—for knowing that asking the boy for his prayers would make the boy feel better about himself—and Mister Rogers responded by looking at me at first with puzzlement and then with surprise. "Oh, heavens no, Tom! I didn't ask him for his prayers for *him*; I asked for me. I asked him because I think that anyone who has gone through challenges like that must be very close to God. I asked him because I wanted his *intercession*."

On December 1, 1997—oh, heck, once upon a time—a boy, no longer little, told his friends to watch out, that he was going to do something "really big" the next day at school, and the next day at school he took his gun and his ammo and his earplugs and shot eight classmates who had clustered for a prayer meeting. Three died, and they were still children, almost. The shootings took place in West Paducah, Kentucky, and when Mister Rogers heard about them, he said, "Oh, wouldn't the world be a different place if he had said, 'I'm going to do something really *little* tomorrow,'" and he decided to dedicate a week of the Neighborhood to the theme "Little and Big." He wanted to tell children that what starts out little can sometimes *become* big, and so they could devote themselves to little dreams without feeling bad about them. But how could Mister Rogers *show* little becoming big, and vice versa? That was a challenge. He couldn't just say it, the way he could always just say to the children who watch his program that they are special to him, or even sing it, the way he would always sing "It's You I Like" and "Everybody's Fancy" and "It's Such a Good Feeling" and "Many Ways to Say I Love You" and "Sometimes People Are Good." No, he had to show it, he had to demonstrate it, and that's how Mister Rogers and the people who work for him eventually got the idea of coming to New York City to visit a woman named Maya Lin.

Maya Lin is a famous architect. Architects are people who create big things from the little designs they draw on pieces of paper. Most famous architects are famous for creating big famous buildings, but Maya Lin is more famous for creating big fancy things for people to look at, and in fact, when Mister Rogers had gone to her studio the day before, he looked at the pictures she had drawn of the clock that is now on the ceiling of a place in New York called Penn Station. A clock is a machine that tells people what time it is, but as Mister Rogers sat in the backseat of an old station wagon hired to take him from his apartment to Penn Station, he worried that Maya Lin's clock might be *too* fancy and that the children who watch the Neighborhood might not understand it. Mister Rogers always worries about things like that, because he always worries about children, and when his station wagon stopped in traffic next to a bus stop, he read aloud the advertisement of an airline trying to push its international service. "Hmmm," Mister Rogers said, *"that's* a strange ad. 'Most people think of us as a great domestic airline. We *hate* that.' Hmmm. *Hate* is such a strong word to use so lightly. If they can hate something like that, you wonder how easy it would be for them to hate something more important." He was with his producer, Margy Whitmer. He had makeup on his face and a dollop of black dye combed into his silver hair. He was wearing beige pants, a blue dress shirt, a tie, dark socks, a pair of dark-blue boating sneakers, and a purple, zippered cardigan. He looked very little in the backseat of the car. Then the car stopped on Thirty-fourth Street, in front of the escalators leading down to the station, and when the doors opened—"Holy s***! It's Mister F***ing Rogers!"—he turned into Mister F***ing Rogers. This was not a bad thing, however, because he was in New York, and in New York it's not an insult to be called Mister F***ing Anything. In fact, it's an honorific. An honorific is what people call you when they respect you, and the moment Mister Rogers got out of the car, people wouldn't stay the f*** away from him, they respected him so much. Oh, Margy Whitmer tried to keep people away from him, tried to tell people that if they gave her their names and addresses, Mister Rogers would send them an autographed picture, but every time she turned around, there was Mister Rogers putting his arms around someone, or wiping the tears off someone's cheek, or passing around the picture of someone's child, or getting on his knees to talk to a child. Margy couldn't stop them, and she couldn't stop him. "Oh, Mister Rogers, thank you for my childhood." "Oh, Mister Rogers, you're the father I never had." "Oh, Mister Rogers, would you please just hug me?" After a while, Margy just rolled her eyes and gave up, because it's always like this with Mister Rogers, because the thing that people don't understand about him is that he's *greedy* for this—greedy for the grace that people offer him. What is grace? He doesn't even know. He can't define it. This is a man who loves the simplifying force of definitions, and yet all he knows of grace is how he gets it; all he knows is that he gets it from God, through man. And so in Penn Station, where he was surrounded by men and women and children, he had this *power*, like a comic-book superhero who absorbs the energy of others until he bursts out of his shirt.

"If Mister F***ing Rogers can tell me how to read that f***ing clock, I'll watch his show every day for a f***ing *year*"—that's what someone in the crowd said while watching Mister Rogers and Maya Lin crane their necks at Maya Lin's big fancy clock, but it didn't even matter whether Mister Rogers could read the clock or not, because every time he looked at it, with the television cameras on him, he leaned back from his waist and opened his mouth wide with astonishment, like someone trying to catch a peanut he had tossed into the air, until it became clear that Mister Rogers could show that he was astonished all *day* if he had to, or even forever, because Mister Rogers lives in a *state* of astonishment, and the astonishment he showed when he looked at the clock was the same astonishment he showed when people—absolute strangers—walked up to him and fed his hungry ear with their whispers, and he turned to me, with an open, abashed mouth, and said, "Oh, Tom, if you could only hear the stories I hear!"

Once upon a time, Mister Rogers went to New York City and got caught in the rain. He didn't have an umbrella, and he couldn't find a taxi, either, so he ducked with a friend into the subway and got on one of the trains. It was late in the day, and the train was crowded with children who were going home from school. Though of all races, the schoolchildren were mostly black and Latino, and they didn't even approach Mister Rogers and ask him for his autograph. They just sang. They sang, all at once, all together, the song he sings at the start of his program, "Won't You Be My Neighbor?" and turned the clattering train into a single soft, runaway choir.

He finds me, of course, at Penn Station. He finds me, because that's what Mister Rogers *does*—he looks, and then he finds. I'm standing against a wall, listening to a bunch of mooks from Long Island discuss the strange word—cariz—a foreign word—he has written down on each of the autographs he gave them. First mook: "He says it's the Greek word for grace." Second mook: "Huh. That's cool. I'm glad I know that. Now, what the f*** is grace?" First mook: "Looks like you're gonna have to break down and buy a dictionary." Second mook: "F*** that. What I'm buying is a ticket to the f***ing *Lotto*. I just met Mister Rogers—this is *definitely* my lucky day." I'm listening to these guys when, from thirty feet away, I notice Mister Rogers looking around for someone and know, immediately, that he is looking for me. He is on one knee in front of a little girl who is hoarding, in her arms, a small stuffed animal, sky-blue, a bunny.

"Remind you of anyone, Tom?" he says when I approach the two of them. He is not speaking of the little girl.

"Yes, Mister Rogers."

"Looks a bit like . . . *Old Rabbit*, doesn't it, Tom?"

"Yes, Mister Rogers."

"I thought so."

Then he turns back to the little girl. "This man's name is Tom. When he was your age, he had a rabbit, too, and he loved it very much. Its name was Old Rabbit. What is yours named?"

The little girl eyes me suspiciously, and then Mister Rogers. She goes a little knock-kneed, directs a thumb toward her mouth. "Bunny Wunny," she says.

"Oh, that's a nice name," Mister Rogers says, and then goes to the Thirty-fourth Street escalator to climb it one last time for the cameras. When he reaches the street, he looks right at the lens, as he always does, and says, speaking of the Neighborhood, "Let's go back to my place," and then makes a right turn toward Seventh Avenue, except that this time he just keeps going, and suddenly Margy Whitmer is saying, "Where is Fred? Where is Fred?" and Fred, he's a hundred yards away, in his sneakers and his purple sweater, and the only thing anyone sees of him is his gray head bobbing up and down amid all the other heads, the hundreds of them, the thousands, the millions, disappearing into the city and its swelter.

Once upon a time, a little boy with a big sword went into battle against Mister Rogers. Or maybe, if the truth be told, Mister Rogers went into battle against a little boy with a big sword, for Mister Rogers didn't *like* the big sword. It was one of those swords that really isn't a sword at all; it was a big plastic contraption with lights and sound effects, and it was the kind of sword used in defense of the universe by the heroes of the television shows that the little boy liked to watch. The little boy with the big sword did not watch Mister Rogers. In fact, the little boy with the big sword didn't know who Mister Rogers *was*, and so when Mister Rogers knelt down in front of him, the little boy with the big sword looked past him and through him, and when Mister Rogers said, "Oh, my, that's a big sword you have," the boy didn't answer, and finally his mother got embarrassed and said, "Oh, honey, c'mon, that's *Mister Rogers*," and felt his head for fever. Of course, she knew who Mister Rogers was, because she had grown up with him, and she knew that he was good for her son, and so now, with her little boy zombie-eyed under his blond bangs, she apologized, saying to Mister Rogers that she knew he was in a rush and that she knew he was here in Penn Station taping his program and that her son usually wasn't *like* this, he was probably just tired. . . . Except that Mister Rogers wasn't going anywhere. Yes, sure, he was taping, and right there, in Penn Station in New York City, were rings of other children wiggling in wait for him, but right now his patient gray eyes were fixed on the little boy with the big sword, and so he stayed there, on one knee, until the little boy's eyes finally focused on Mister Rogers, and he said, "It's not a sword; it's a death ray." A death ray! Oh, honey, Mommy *knew* you could do it. . . . And so now, encouraged, Mommy said, "Do you want to give Mister Rogers a hug, honey?" But the boy was shaking his head no, and Mister Rogers was sneaking his face past the big sword and the armor of the little boy's eyes and whispering something in his ear— something that, while not changing his mind about the hug, made the little boy look at Mister Rogers in a new way, with the eyes of a child at last, and nod his head yes.

We were heading back to his apartment in a taxi when I asked him what he had said.

"Oh, I just knew that whenever you see a little boy carrying something like that, it means that he wants to show people that he's strong on the outside. I just wanted to let him know that he was strong on the inside, too. And so that's what I told him. I said, 'Do you know that you're strong on the inside, too?' Maybe it was something he needed to hear."

———————

He was barely more than a boy himself when he learned what he would be fighting for, and fighting against, for the rest of his life. He was in college. He was a music major at a small school in Florida and planning to go to seminary upon graduation. His name was Fred Rogers. He came home to Latrobe, Pennsylvania, once upon a time, and his parents, because they were wealthy, had bought something new for the corner room of their big redbrick house. It was a television. Fred turned it on, and as he says now, with plaintive distaste, "there were people throwing *pies* at one another." He was the soft son of overprotective parents, but he believed, right then, that he was strong enough to enter into battle with *that*—that machine, that medium—and to wrestle with it until it yielded to him, until the ground touched by its blue shadow became hallowed and this thing called television came to be used "for the broadcasting of grace through the land." It would not be easy, no—for in order to win such a battle, he would have to forbid himself the privilege of stopping, and whatever he did right he would have to repeat, as though he were already living in eternity. And so it was that the puppets he employed on *The Children's Corner* would be the puppets he employed forty-four years later, and so it was that once he took off his jacket and his shoes . . . well, he was Mister Rogers for good. And even now, when he is producing only three weeks' worth of new programs a year, he still winds up agonizing—*agonizing*—about whether to announce his theme as "Little and Big" or "Big and Little" and still makes only two edits per televised minute, because he doesn't want his message to be determined by the cuts and splices in a piece of tape—to become, despite all his fierce coherence, "a message of fragmentation."

He is losing, of course. The revolution he started—a half hour a day, five days a week—it wasn't enough, it didn't *spread*, and so, forced to fight his battles alone, Mister Rogers is losing, as we all are losing. He is losing to it, to *our* twenty-four-hour-a-day pie fight, to the dizzying cut and the disorienting edit, to the message of fragmentation, to the flicker and pulse and shudder and strobe, to the constant, hivey drone of the electroculture . . . and yet still he fights, deathly afraid that the medium he chose is consuming the very things he tried to protect: childhood and silence. Yes, at seventy years old and 143 pounds, Mister Rogers still fights, and indeed, early this year, when television handed him its highest honor, he responded by telling television—gently, of course—to just *shut up* for once, and television listened. He had already won his third Daytime Emmy, and now he went onstage to accept Emmy's Lifetime Achievement Award, and there, in front of all the soap-opera stars and talk-show sinceratrons, in front of all the jutting man-tanned jaws and jutting saltwater bosoms, he made his small bow and said into the microphone, "All of us have special ones who have loved us into being. Would you just take, along with me, *ten seconds* to think of the people who have helped you become who you are. . . . Ten seconds of silence." And then he lifted his wrist, and looked at the audience, and looked at his watch, and said softly, "I'll watch the time," and there was, at first, a small whoop from the crowd, a giddy, strangled hiccup of laughter, as people realized that *he wasn't kidding*, that Mister Rogers was not some convenient eunuch but rather a *man*, an authority figure who actually expected them to do what he asked . . . and so they did. One second, two seconds, three seconds . . . and now the jaws clenched, and the bosoms heaved, and the mascara ran, and the tears fell upon the beglittered gathering like rain leaking down a crystal chandelier, and Mister Rogers finally looked up from his watch and said, "May God be with you" to all his vanquished children.

Once upon a time, there was a little boy born blind, and so, defenseless in the world, he suffered the abuses of the defenseless, and when he grew up and became a man, he looked back and realized that he'd had no childhood at all, and that if he were ever to have a childhood, he would have to start having it now, in his forties. So the first thing he did was rechristen himself "Joybubbles"; the second thing he did was declare himself five years old forever; and the third thing he did was make a pilgrimage to Pittsburgh, where the University of Pittsburgh's Information Sciences Library keeps a Mister Rogers archive. It has all 865 programs, in both color and black and white, and for two months this past spring, Joybubbles went to the library every day for ten hours and watched the Neighborhood's every episode, plus specials—or, since he is blind, *listened* to every episode, *imagined* every episode. Until one night, Mister Rogers came to him, in what he calls a visitation—"I was dreaming, but I was awake"—and offered to teach him how to pray.

"But Mister Rogers, I can't pray," Joybubbles said, "because every time I try to pray, I forget the words."

"I know that," Mister Rogers said, "and that's why the prayer I'm going to teach you has only three words."

"What prayer is that, Mister Rogers? What kind of prayer has only three words?"

"Thank you, God," Mister Rogers said.

The walls of Mister Rogers' Neighborhood are light blue and fleeced with clouds. They are tall—as tall as the cinder-block walls they are designed to hide—and they encompass the Neighborhood's entire stage set, from the flimsy yellow house where Mister Rogers comes to visit, to the closet where he finds his sweaters, to the Neighborhood of Make-Believe, where he goes to dream. The blue walls are the ends of the daylit universe he has made, and yet Mister Rogers can't *see* them—or at least can't know them—because he was born blind to color. He doesn't know the color of his walls, and one day, when I caught him looking toward his painted skies, I asked him to tell me what color they *are*, and he said, "I imagine they're *blue*, Tom." Then he looked at me and smiled. "I imagine they're blue."

He has spent thirty-one years imagining and reimagining those walls—the walls that have both penned him in and set him free. You would think it would be easy by now, being Mister Rogers; you would think that one morning he would wake up and think, Okay, all I have to do is be *nice* for my allotted half hour today, and then I'll just take the rest of the day off. . . . But no,

Mister Rogers is a stubborn man, and so on the day I ask about the color of his sky, he has already gotten up at five-thirty, already prayed for those who have asked for his prayers, already read, already written, already swum, already weighed himself, already sent out cards for the birthdays he never forgets, already called any number of people who depend on him for comfort, already cried when he read the letter of a mother whose child was buried with a picture of Mister Rogers in his casket, already played for twenty minutes with an autistic boy who has come, with his father, all the way from Boise, Idaho, to meet him. The boy had never spoken, until one day he said, "X the Owl," which is the name of one of Mister Rogers's puppets, and he had never looked his father in the eye until one day his father had said, "Let's go to the Neighborhood of Make-Believe," and now the boy is speaking and reading, and the father has come to thank Mister Rogers for saving his son's life. . . . And by this time, well, it's nine-thirty in the morning, time for Mister Rogers to take off his jacket and his shoes and put on his sweater and his sneakers and start taping another visit to the Neighborhood. He writes all his own scripts, but on this day, when he receives a visit from Mrs. McFeely and a springer spaniel, she says that she has to bring the dog "back to his owner," and Mister Rogers makes a face. The cameras stop, and he says, "I don't like the word owner there. It's not a good word. Let's change it to 'bring the dog *home*.'" And so the change is made, and the taping resumes, and this is how it goes all day, a life unfolding within a clasp of unfathomable governance, and once, when I lose sight of him, I ask Margy Whitmer where he is, and she says, "Right over your shoulder, where he always is," and when I turn around, Mister Rogers is facing me, child-stealthy, with a small black camera in his hand, to take another picture for the album that he will give me when I take my leave of him.

Yes, it should be easy being Mister Rogers, but when four o'clock rolls around, well, Mister Rogers is *tired*, and so he sneaks over to the piano and starts playing, with dexterous, pale fingers, the music that used to end a 1940s newsreel and that has now become the music he plays to signal to the cast and crew that a day's taping has wrapped. On this day, however, he is premature by a considerable extent, and so Margy, who has been with Mister Rogers since 1983—because nobody who works for Mister Rogers ever *leaves* the Neighborhood—comes running over, papers in hand, and says, "Not so fast there, buster."

"Oh, please, sister," Mister Rogers says. "I'm done."

And now Margy comes up behind him and massages his shoulders. "No, you're not," she says. "Roy Rogers is done. Mister Rogers still has a ways to go."

He was a child, once, too, and so one day I asked him if I could go with him back to Latrobe. He thought about it for a second, then said, by way of agreement, "Okay, then—tomorrow, Tom, I'll show you childhood." Not *his* childhood, mind you, or even *a* childhood—no, just "childhood." And so the next morning, we swam together, and then he put on his boxer shorts and the dark socks, and the T-shirt, and the gray trousers, and the belt, and then the white dress shirt and the black bow tie and the gray suit jacket, and about two hours later we were pulling up to the big brick house on Weldon Street in Latrobe, and Mister Rogers was thinking about going inside.

There was nobody home. The doors were open, unlocked, because the house was undergoing a renovation of some kind, but the owners were away, and Mister Rogers's boyhood home was empty of everyone but workmen. "Do you think we can go in?" he asked Bill Isler, president of Family Communications, the company that produces *Mister Rogers' Neighborhood*. Bill had driven us there, and now, sitting behind the wheel of his red Grand Cherokee, he was full of remonstrance. "No!" he said. "Fred, they're *not home*. If we wanted to go into the house, we should have *called* first. Fred . . ." But Mister Rogers was out of the car, with his camera in his hand and his legs moving so fast that the material of his gray suit pants furled and unfurled around both of his skinny legs, like flags exploding in a breeze. And here, as he made his way through thickets of bewildered workmen—this skinny old man dressed in a gray suit and a bow tie, with his hands on his hips and his arms akimbo, like a dance instructor—there was some kind of wiggly jazz in his legs, and he went flying all around the outside of the house, pointing at windows, saying there was the room where he learned to play the piano, and there was the room where he saw the pie fight on a primitive television, and there was the room where his beloved father died . . . until finally we reached the front door. He put his hand on the knob; he cracked it open, but then, with Bill Isler calling caution from the car, he said, "Maybe we *shouldn't* go in. And all the people who made this house special to me are not here, anyway. They're all in heaven."

And so we went to the graveyard. We were heading there all along, because Mister Rogers *loves* graveyards, and so as we took the long, straight road out of sad, fading Latrobe, you could still feel the *speed* in him, the hurry, as he mustered up a sad anticipation, and when we passed through the cemetery gates, he smiled as he said to Bill Isler, "The plot's at the end of the yellow-brick road." And so it was; the asphalt ended, and then we began bouncing over a road of old blond bricks, until even that road ended, and we were parked in front of the place where Mister Rogers is to be buried. He got out of the car, and, moving as quickly as he had moved to the door of his house, he stepped up a small hill to the door of a large gray mausoleum, a huge structure built for six, with a slightly peaked roof, and bronze doors, and angels living in the stained glass. He peeked in the window, and in the same voice he uses on television, *that* voice, at once so patient and so eager, he pointed out each crypt, saying "There's my father, and there's my mother, and there, on the left, is my place, and right across will be Joanne. . . ." The window was of darkened glass, though, and so to see through it, we had to press our faces close against it, and where the glass had warped away from the frame of the door—where there was a finger-wide crack—Mister Rogers's voice leaked into his grave, and came back to us as a soft, hollow echo.

And then he was on the move again, happily, quickly, for he would not leave until he showed me all the places of all those who'd loved him into being. His grandfather, his grandmother, his uncles, his aunts, his father-in-law and mother-in-law, even his family's servants—he went to each grave, and spoke their names, and told their stories, until finally I headed back down to the Jeep and turned back around to see Mister Rogers standing high on a green dell, smiling among the stones. "And now if you don't mind," he said without a hint of shame or embarrassment, "I have to find a place to relieve myself," and then off he went, this ecstatic ascetic, to take a proud piss in his corner of heaven.

Once upon a time, a man named Fred Rogers decided that he wanted to live in heaven. Heaven is the place where good people go when they die, but this man, Fred Rogers, didn't want to *go* to heaven; he wanted to *live* in heaven, here, now, in this world, and so one day, when he was talking about all the people he had loved in this life, he looked at me and said, "The connections we make in the course of a life—maybe that's what heaven is, Tom. We make so *many* connections here on earth. Look at us—I've just met you, but I'm investing in who you are and who you will be, and I can't help it."

The next afternoon, I went to his office in Pittsburgh. He was sitting on a couch, under a framed rendering of the Greek word for grace and a biblical phrase written in Hebrew that means "I am my beloved's, and my beloved is mine." A woman was with him, sitting in a big chair. Her name was Deb. She was very pretty. She had a long face and a dark blush to her skin. She had curls in her hair and stars at the centers of her eyes. She was a minister at Fred Rogers's church. She spent much of her time tending to the sick and the dying. Fred Rogers loved her very much, and so, out of nowhere, he smiled and put his hand over hers. "Will you be with me when I die?" he asked her, and when she said yes, he said, "Oh, thank you, my dear." Then, with his hand still over hers and his eyes looking straight into hers, he said, "Deb, do you know what a great prayer you are? Do you know that about yourself? Your prayers are just wonderful." Then he looked at me. I was sitting in a small chair by the door, and he said, "Tom, would you close the door, please?" I closed the door and sat back down. "Thanks, my dear," he said to me, then turned back to Deb. "Now, Deb, I'd like to ask you a favor," he said. "Would you lead us? Would you lead us in prayer?"

Deb stiffened for a second, and she let out a breath, and her color got deeper. "Oh, I don't know, Fred," she said. "I don't know if I want to put on a *performance....*"

Fred never stopped looking at her or let go of her hand. "It's not a performance. It's just a meeting of friends," he said. He moved his hand from her wrist to her palm and extended his other hand to me. I took it and then put my hand around her free hand. His hand was warm, hers was cool, and we bowed our heads, and closed our eyes, and I heard Deb's voice calling out for the grace of God. What is grace? I'm not certain; all I know is that my heart felt like a spike, and then, in that room, it opened and felt like an umbrella. I had never prayed like that before, ever. I had always been a great prayer, a powerful one, but only fitfully, only out of guilt, only when fear and desperation drove me to it . . . and it hit me, right then, with my eyes closed, that this was the moment Fred Rogers—Mister Rogers—had been leading me to from the moment he answered the door of his apartment in his bathrobe and asked me about Old Rabbit. Once upon a time, you see, I lost something, and prayed to get it back, but when I lost it the second time, I didn't, and now this was it, the missing word, the unuttered promise, the prayer I'd been waiting to say a very long time.

"Thank you, God," Mister Rogers said.

A

BEAUTIFUL DAY

in the

NEIGHBORHOOD

DEAR READER:

"What is essential is invisible to the eye."

What does that mean to you?

That saying is framed and sits on a table right beside me in my Neighborhood office. Everyone who sees those words from Saint-Exupéry's *The Little Prince* reads them with his or her own eyes . . . and with what's invisible and essential behind those eyes. Just like with the passages in this book, you will bring your own experiences, your own beliefs, to every page. That's what will enrich these words beyond measure.

The ideas in this collection have come from things that I have learned and thought about for a long time. They come, too, from many people whom I have met along the way. I've been fortunate to have had some extraordinary teachers who have given me some powerful words that helped me learn about life and about childhood. One of those teachers was my grandfather, the one I'm named for: Fred Brooks McFeely. He wasn't a teacher by training, but he taught me through his love. Because he cared so much about me, I wanted to learn from him. I can still remember his saying to me, "Freddy, I like you, just the way you are." That quotation meant so much to me that I've often shared it with our television viewers. Those Neighborhood words have very deep roots in my own childhood!

Communication for me has always been more than words. When I was just five, I found I could easily express my feelings through my fingers at the piano. And as an adult I find writing the melodies and the lyrics for our *Neighborhood* program has been a very important way for me to express a wide range of human emotions.

When I headed for college, I decided to work on a degree in music composition. It was during my senior year at Rollins College, in the early 1950s, that I first saw television. I was appalled by what were labeled "children's programs"—pies in faces and slapstick! That's when I decided to go into this field. Children deserve better. Children need better.

My first television job was in 1951. I was a floor manager for the network music programs at NBC in New York for two years. When WQED (Pittsburgh's public television station) was getting started, I was invited to come back to my hometown area of western Pennsylvania to co-produce an hour-long live daily program for young people called *The Children's Corner* with Josie Carey. I was also the behind-the-scenes puppeteer and organist.

To deepen what I could bring to television, I added seminary studies for eight years during my lunch hours and evenings. At my ordination as a Presbyterian minister, I was given a special charge to serve children and their families through the mass media.

Knowing my great interest in children, one of my seminary professors suggested I meet Dr. Margaret McFarland. She was the director of the Arsenal Family and Children's Center of the University of Pittsburgh. The noted psychologist Erik Erikson, who helped found that center, has said that Margaret knew more than anyone in this world about families with young children.

Margaret became my mentor when I began graduate studies in child development. It was natural that we would invite her to be our chief psychological consultant for *Mister Rogers' Neighborhood*. She generously carried out that duty for almost twenty-five years. Her death in 1988 was one of the major losses I've had to deal with in my life. It was she who helped me think about the child who grew inside of me. It was Margaret who helped me really *listen* to children so that I could discover who they were and what was important in their lives, so that my communication with them through television could be meaningful. That kind of invisible "essential" is a gift nothing can ever take away . . . not even death.

I care deeply about communication, about words—what we say and what we hear.

While our television communication might look simple to some, it really isn't. Children are not simple . . . neither are adults. I have always given a great deal of thought to how I present ideas during our television visits, and I'm always fascinated to hear how people have used what we have said—on television, in speeches, during interviews, and in our books. Often they've used our ideas in creative, productive ways I had never dreamed they could be used.

So may it be with the words in this book, which have been gathered from my speeches, songs, newspaper columns, books, and television programs. Once you've read them and made them your own, may they find their place in the innermost part of you—in that essential part of you that inspires you to be who you really are.

—FRED ROGERS

CHAPTER ONE

You Are Special

It's you I like,
It's not the things you wear,
It's not the way you do your hair—
But it's you I like.

The way you are right now,
The way down deep inside you—
Not the things that hide you,
Not your toys—
They're just beside you.

But it's you I like,
Every part of you,
Your skin, your eyes, your feelings
Whether old or new.
I hope that you'll remember
Even when you're feeling blue
That it's you I like,
It's you yourself, it's you,
It's you . . . I . . . like!

> —FROM THE SONG "IT'S YOU I LIKE"

✧ There's only one person in the whole world like you. If you think about it for a moment, there never has been . . . and there never will be—in the history of the earth—another person just like you.

✧ We're all so much alike . . . and yet we're all so different! I find myself rejoicing at the endless variety of human beings, and that's partly, I know, because your differences from one another tell me that it's all right for me to be different in many ways, too.

✧ I really think that everybody, every day, should be able to feel some success.

✧ Being perfectly human means having imperfections. All the same, most of us strive mightily to be perfectly lovable in the eyes of those we love. What those eyes tell us while we are infants are the most important messages we get about the value of being who we are.

✧ Nothing can replace the influence of unconditional love in the life of a child.

❖ In the disappointment of a defeat, a child may seem to find little comfort in our saying, "But you really tried hard, and I'm proud of you." It takes time to get over a disappointment. For those children who have learned to feel valued and loved by the people they love, these disappointments do pass. It's the children who are less fortunate, those who feel they have to bank everything on their performance, who come to believe that losing in a competition means being one of life's unloved "losers."

❖ When we love a person, we accept him or her exactly as is: the lovely with the unlovely, the strong along with the fearful, the true mixed in with the façade, and of course, the only way we can do it is by accepting ourselves that way.

❖ Little by little we human beings are confronted with situations that give us more and more clues that we aren't perfect.

❖ We all need to feel that we have gifts to give that are acceptable and valued.

❖ My good friend Emilie Jacobson, who was the "Poetry Lady" on our television programs for many years, helped us all to feel good about who we were. She often quoted a poem by Douglas

Malloch, and it became her trademark. Here are the first and last verses:

> If you can't be a pine on the top of a hill,
> Be a scrub in the valley, but be
> The best little scrub by the side of the rill,
> Be a bush if you can't be a tree.
>
> If you can't be a highway, then just be a trail.
> If you can't be a sun, be a star.
> It isn't by size that you win or you fail.
> Be the best of whatever you are.

✧ We serve children best when we try to find out what their own inner needs are and what their own unique endowments are, and to help them capitalize on that.

✧ It's what's inside us that matters most.

✧ The people who care about you can like you just because you're you.

❧ Shyness isn't something that just children feel. Anybody can feel shy. And one reason we feel that way is that we're not sure other people will like us just the way we are.

❧ No child is "perfectly" whole in mind, body, spirit, ability . . . nor can any child meet all of a parent's hopes and expectations. Yet there is a wholeness of each and every child, a wholeness that is unique and that brings with it a unique set of possibilities and limitations, a unique set of opportunities for fulfillment.

❧ You can't really love someone else unless you really love yourself first.

❧ One of the strongest things I have had to wrestle with in my life is the significance of the longing for perfection in oneself and in the people bound to the self by friendship or parenthood or childhood.

❧ What matters most is how children feel about their uniqueness once they do begin to realize that they are different from everyone else. How each one of us comes to feel about our individual uniqueness has a strong influence on how we feel about everyone's uniqueness—whether we grow into adults who rejoice in the diversity of the world's people or into adults who fear and resent that diversity.

❖ There's probably no way we can keep our children from feeling sad or angry when they lose, any more than we can keep ourselves from feeling that way. What we can help them understand, though, is that though we appreciate them for what they do, we love them even more for who they are. We can let them know, too, that if they win or lose, we will always be proud of them for doing the best they can.

❖ We all have different gifts, so we all have different ways of saying to the world who we are.

❖ Deep within us—no matter who we are—there lives a feeling of wanting to be lovable, of wanting to be the kind of person that others like to be with.

❖ Children do not develop in a healthy way unless they have the feeling that they are needed—that they enhance the life of someone else, that they have value apart from anything that they own or any skill that they learn.

❖ Everyone longs to be loved. And the greatest thing we can do is to let people know that they are loved and capable of loving.

❖ What concerns me most these days are those people who think that we must (or even *can*) bypass feelings in order to develop the great national resource called children.

❖ The greatest loss that we all have to deal with is the loss of the image of ourself as a perfect person.

❖ What's been important in my understanding of myself and others is the fact that each one of us is so much more than any one thing. A sick child is much more than his or her sickness. A person with a disability is much, much more than a handicap. A pediatrician is more than a medical doctor. You're *much* more than your job description or your age or your income or your output.

❖ Children can't be expected to leave the unhappy and angry parts of themselves at the door before coming in. We all need to feel that we can bring the whole of ourselves to the people who care about us.

❖ The world needs a sense of worth, and it will achieve it only by its people feeling that they are worthwhile.

❖ Only by understanding our own uniqueness can we fully appreciate how special our neighbor really is. Only by being aware of our own endowments can we begin to marvel at the variety that our Creator has provided in humankind.

❖ We reason that if we're perfect, if we do a perfect job, we will receive perfect love! We further believe that if we're not perfect (and of course, no one is), we might lose the love of people who mean the most to us.

❖ If you could only sense how important you are to the lives of those you meet; how important you can be to people you may never even dream of. There is something of yourself that you leave at every meeting with another person.

❖ Each person in the world is a unique human being, and each has unique human potential. One of the important tasks of growing up is the *discovery* of this uniqueness: the discovery of "who I am" in each of us—of "who I am" in relationship to all those whom I meet.

❧ Nobody knows what you're thinking or feeling unless you share it. Whatever we choose to imagine can be as private as we want it to be. No one can know what it is unless we want to tell someone about it.

❧ It's your very being that I like, not all the facts that you learn in school or all the things that people buy for you to wear or play with. It's your *self* that means so much to me.

❧ You can't be a winner all the time.

❧ One of the mysteries is that as unlike as we are, one human being from another, we also share much in common. Our lives begin the same way, by birth. The love and interdependence of parents and children is universal, and so are the many difficulties parents and children have in becoming separate from one another. As we grow, we laugh and cry at many of the same things, and fear many of the same things. At the end, we all leave the same way— by death. Yet no two threads—no two lives—in that vast tapestry of existence have ever been, or ever will be, the same.

✧ It's the people who feel strong and good about themselves inside who are best able to accept outside differences—their own or others'. We help children develop this ability every time we affirm how special they are to us for being themselves, and how special to us are all the things that make each person different from anyone else.

✧ A sense of individual identity is one of the greatest gifts that parents can give a child. If that gift is not given, children will have to fight for their identities instead. When twins have to fight each other for it, they could, indeed, grow up to be "identical strangers."

✧ As human beings, our job in life is to help people realize how rare and valuable each one of us really is, that each of us has something that no one else has—or ever will have—something inside that is unique to all time. It's our job to encourage each other to discover that uniqueness and to provide ways of developing its expression.

✧ Uniqueness and children's feelings about it can't take on full meaning in children's lives unless they also come to understand how much we are all alike. Finding out that we are one of a kind could be a lonely and frightening thing without the reassurance of knowing that we belong to humankind . . . and that all humans laugh and cry about many of the same things; that all have similar hopes and fears; that all have many of the same needs; and that those needs are best met by other human beings who can love us for both our similarities and our differences.

✧ Young boys and girls don't really want their mothers and fathers all to themselves all the time, but they do long for the feeling of being best loved and most beautiful and specially prized *at least some of the time.*

✧ Superheroes are fascinating to many children, and we can help them know it's not an imaginary superself, but each person's *real* self, that does the really important things in life. As we give importance to what they're learning to do when they're little, we can also assure them that as they grow, they will be able to accomplish other important things, too.

❖ The roots of a child's ability to cope and thrive, regardless of circumstance, lie in that child's having had at least a small, safe place (an apartment? a room? a lap?) in which, in the companionship of a loving person, that child could discover that he or she was lovable and capable of loving in return.

❖ All people share many of the same feelings, have many of the same hopes, and suffer many of the same disappointments. And everyone needs to feel lovable and capable of loving. Those seem to be common roots that humans share, and feeling good about this is an important step toward a child's good feelings about his or her uniqueness and the diversity of others.

❖ I like you just the way you are.

CHAPTER TWO

Relationships

It's the people you like the most
Who can make you feel maddest.
It's the people you care for the most
Who manage to make you feel baddest.

It's the people you like the most
Who can make you feel happiest!
It's the people you care for the most, most
      likely,
Who manage to make you feel snappiest!

—FROM THE SONG
   "IT'S THE PEOPLE YOU LIKE THE MOST"

❧ Love isn't a state of perfect caring. It is an active noun like "struggle." To love someone is to strive to accept that person exactly the way he or she is, right here and now—and to go on caring even through times that may bring us pain.

❧ Helen Ross was a good friend who taught teachers, doctors, and psychiatrists and consulted with professionals working with children and families all over the world. She was one of the great people of our age in the understanding of the dynamic development of human beings. After one operation for cancer and some subsequent therapy, Helen chose to refuse treatment when the cancer reappeared. One day when I visited her, I found Helen very frail yet interested in all that I had to tell her about our television work and her Pittsburgh friends. Some of the time I just held her hand, and we said nothing. We didn't have to. After one of those silences, Helen said to me, "Do you ever pray for people, Fred?" "Of course I do." I simply said, "Dear God, encircle us with Thy love wherever we may be." And Helen replied, "That's what it is, isn't it?—it's love. That's what it's all about." Helen was eighty-eight when she died. She had spent most of her adult life working at understanding the complexities of human growth and development, and her summation of life is that love is what it's all about. It meant a lot to me to hear that from her.

❖ As you continue to work on your understanding of your self and others, you are really engaged in love.

❖ Children take their parents' opinions and their teachers' opinions *very* seriously, so honesty linked with love is the most important response in any relationship.

❖ We need to help people discover the true meaning of love. Love is generally confused with dependence. Those of us who have grown in true love know that we can love only in proportion to our capacity for independence.

❖ An ability to accept our ambivalence toward others may be an important ingredient in relationships that are healthy and lasting.

❖ It's the people we love the most who can make us feel the gladdest . . . and the maddest! Love and anger are such a puzzle! It's hard enough for us, as adults, to understand and manage our angry feelings toward parents, spouses, and children, or to keep their anger toward us in perspective. It's a different kind of anger from the kind we may feel toward strangers because it is so deeply intertwined with caring and attachment.

✧ A friend of mine made a calligraphy scroll that I have framed in my writing room. It reads: "The greatest gift one can give to another person is a deeper understanding of life and the ability to love and believe in the self."

✧ Mutually caring relationships require kindness and patience, tolerance, optimism, joy in the other's achievements, confidence in oneself, and the ability to give without undue thought of gain. We need to accept the fact that it's not in the power of any human being to provide all these things all the time. For any of us, mutually caring relationships will also always include some measure of unkindness and impatience, intolerance, pessimism, envy, self-doubt, and disappointment.

✧ Listening is a very active awareness of the coming together of at least two lives. Listening, as far as I'm concerned, is certainly a prerequisite of love. One of the most essential ways of saying "I love you" is by being a receptive listener.

✧ Love is like infinity. You can't have more or less infinity, and you can't compare two things to see if they're equally infinite. Infinity just is, and that's the way I think love is, too.

Have you had people who have touched you—not moved you in order to manipulate you—but touched you inside-to-inside? Take a minute to think of at least one person who helped you to become who you are *inside* today. Someone who was interested in you for who you really are . . . someone you feel really accepted the essence of your being. Just one minute . . . one minute to think of those who have made a real difference in your life.

❖ Relationships are like dances in which people try to find whatever happens to be the mutual rhythm in their lives.

❖ Something we all need in order to feel the fullness of life: It's not only a sense that we belong on our planet, but also that we belong in other people's lives—that we are loved, lovable, and capable of loving.

❖ The toughest thing is to love somebody who has done something mean to you . . . especially when that somebody has been yourself. Look inside yourself and find that loving part of you. Take good care of that part because that part helps you love your neighbor.

❖ There are some people who can't say the words "I love you," but they sure can let you know that they love you.

❖ It may be easier for us if, as children, we were allowed to have our angry feelings and if someone we loved let us know that those feelings were a normal part of loving and being loved. It will certainly have helped us if we learned to talk about those feelings and express them in healthy ways.

One of my wise teachers, Dr. Orr, told me, "There is only one thing evil cannot stand, and that is forgiveness."

⊹ A person can grow to his or her fullest capacity only in mutually caring relationships with others.

⊹ Honesty in love is often very hard. The truth is often painful. But the freedom it can bring is worth the trying.

⊹ Feeling good about ourselves is essential in our being able to love others.

⊹ Losing trust is a frightful thing. And regaining it must come through an atmosphere of love—no other way but through love.

⊹ You bring all you ever were and are to any relationship you have today.

⊹ There are so many people who feel that witnessing somebody acting out destructive aggressions is healthy. I don't agree. I feel we can encourage people to do things that can become constructive, to do things with their hands and feelings that don't need to be destructive.

✧ Caring comes from the Gothic word *kara*, which means "to lament." So caring is not what a powerful person gives to a weaker one. Caring is a matter of being there . . . lamenting right along with the one who laments.

✧ Taking care is one way to show your love. Another way is letting people take good care of you when you need it.

✧ The values we care about the deepest and the movements within society that support those values command our love—and when those things that we care about so deeply become endangered, we become enraged. And what a healthy thing that is! Without it, we would never stand up and speak out for what we believe.

✧ It's a mistake to think that we have to be lovely to be loved by human beings or by God.

✧ It's no secret that I like to get to know people—and not just the outside stuff of their lives. I like to try to understand the meaning of who people are and what they're saying to me.

❖ A parent can be both loving and angry.

❖ As a marriage matures, you start to see that just being there for each other is the most important thing you can do, just being there to listen and to be sorry or happy with him or her, to share all that there is to share.

❖ My hunch is that anyone who has ever been able to sustain good work has had at least one person—and often many—who have believed in him or her. We just don't get to be competent human beings without a lot of different investments from others.

❖ In the infant, love and rage are fused—they're both just part of feeling. If a baby's needs are taken care of, he or she feels good, feels loving. If needs are not provided for, the baby feels bad and out-raged. Little by little, though, we healthy human beings do grow to be able to tell the difference between our love and our rage. We can tell someone "I love you," and we can tell someone "I'm angry with you."

❖ Anger makes us feel so isolated.

❧ Loving has a lot to do with giving and receiving. Often, it is so much easier to give than to receive because when we give we are in a position of control, but when we receive, we are asked to receive what is given to us.

❧ There's a nurturing element to all human beings (whenever they themselves have been nurtured), and it's going to be expressed or repressed, one or the other. Whether we're male or female, if we have been cared for by another, we have within us the capacity to give care.

❧ What children are really afraid of when they're angry is that they're going to hurt somebody, particularly somebody they love. And it's really scary because they just feel overcome with rage.

❧ "What do you do with the mad that you feel when you feel so mad you could bite?" was a question that a child really did ask a doctor one day. When I heard it, it reminded me how intense children's anger can be—and how hard for them to cope with and understand.

✧ It is natural for parents to feel different about each of their children, and I don't believe that recognizing our different feelings need bring us guilt. But as for love, it's there or it isn't. That may be the most one can hope to say, and when it is there . . . well, that's saying more than enough.

✧ It's through human relationships that a child first learns love, compassion, generosity, and creativity.

CHAPTER THREE

Childhood

You used to creep and crawl real well
But then you learned to walk real well.
There was a time you'd coo and cry
But then you learned to talk and, my!
You almost always try.
You almost always do your best.
I like the way you're growing up,
It's fun, that's all.

You're growing, you're growing,
You're growing in and out . . .

—FROM THE SONG "YOU'RE GROWING"

✧ Childhood isn't just something we "get through." It's a big journey, and it's one we've all taken. Most likely, though, we've forgotten how much we had to learn along the way about ourselves and others.

✧ My own wish for children is that they learn to find joy even amidst the world's and their own imperfections, that they grow to have a clear but forgiving interior voice to guide them, and that they come to have a reasonable sense of shame without unreasonable burdens of guilt.

✧ Every child spends the first years of life discovering his or her separateness and individuality. There are the tasks of learning how our bodies work and what our relationships are to the people and the world around us. We have to learn what's real and what's fantasy, how to understand and express our feelings, how people are alike and how they are different. And, of course, all children have to learn how to wait, share, try . . . and cope with disappointment and loss.

✧ All of our growth is rooted in the firm trust that all of those who first cared about us maintained.

✧ Healthy babies grow from one phase to another in a predictable way. Human beings have to learn to crawl before they learn to walk. And when we're ready to crawl, we'll find every chance we can to crawl and crawl and crawl—and we don't want people to stop us from crawling, and we don't want people to hurry us to walk. There is an inner rhythm that sets the normal beat for human growth. We need to respect that rhythm in ourselves, our friends, and the children with whom we live and work.

✧ It is normal for children to have all sorts of fears as they grow, and it's normal for these fears to take the shape of imaginary creatures or people.

✧ As babies, we're completely dependent on what other people do to and for us. Most of what we are learning then about ourselves and our world comes through other people, and part of what we have to learn as we go is how to adapt to these people while still remaining the individuals we are.

✧ Like many other values our children get from us, compassion is more likely to be caught than taught.

✧ A two-year-old is not a six-year-old, and a six-year-old is not an adult! That may seem like a simplistic statement, but I've seen people in all walks of life treat some two-year-olds as if they were six-year-olds, and some six-year-olds as if they were adults.

✧ Learning to expect the return of the people they love is a major task in all children's ability to tolerate those people's periodic absences.

✧ Most of us, I believe, admire strength. It's something we tend to respect in others, desire for ourselves, and wish for our children. Sometimes, though, I wonder if we confuse strength with other words—like aggression and even violence.

✧ Children have a wonderful way of discerning the truth . . . even when we think it's being hidden.

✧ Somewhere early on, I got the idea inside of me that childhood was valuable, that children were worthy of being seen *and* heard, and who they were had a lot to do with how our world would become.

✧ There is much more to independence than learning to master new skills. One of the most important parts of independence is learning to form new relationships with other people.

✧ "Hungry hands"—that's what Dr. McFarland liked to call the way toddlers want to put their hands on everything. There's a scene in an old home movie taken when I was a toddler, in which I'm in my father's arms. He's trying to put his hat on my head, but each time he does, I snatch it off and throw it down. There must be scenes like that in countless home movies and home videos everywhere. My hands were certainly "hungry" in that scene. They couldn't wait to get hold of that hat—and get rid of it. What was remarkable was that my hands could do so. Only a few months before, I would not have been able to put together the feeling that I didn't like the hat on my head, the intention to take it off, and the coordination needed for my hands to do so. A few months before that, I wouldn't have known even what or where my hands were to begin with.

✧ Thumb-sucking can be one of the first ways infants begin learning that the outermost parts of their bodies are actually attached to them, and that they can give themselves comfort while feeling hungry and waiting to be fed.

❖ One of the universal fears of childhood is the fear of not hav-ing value in the eyes of the people whom we admire so much.

❖ Children do wish for things, and if they wish for something terrible to happen to someone they love, and it does happen, they may be left with deep-seated and long-lasting feelings of responsi-bility and guilt. They need to know that even scary, mad wishes don't make things come true, and it's that part of wishing that I think children do need to understand right away.

❖ It can take confidence to grow, and there are times when chil-dren need to borrow that confidence from the people they love and want to please.

❖ As children develop in their own ways as individuals, and as sons and daughters, and as brothers and sisters or playmates, there's a dance going on. To borrow a phrase from the writer An-thony Powell, it's a "dance to the music of time." That dance has its own rhythms. The steps to that dance can be made more comfort-able, easier to learn, but they can't be hurried.

❖ Children's fantasies about the unknown are often much more frightening than the reality itself.

❖ Young children naturally imagine their parents to know everything about them. But as we grow, we learn there is an inner privacy of self. There is no one who sees all, hears all, and knows all about any one of us. Who we are inside and what we do alone is our own business. Who we choose to tell and what we choose to tell is our own business, too.

❖ The world is not always a kind place. That's something all children learn for themselves, whether we want them to or not, but it's something they really need our help to understand.

❖ Just because a child's behavior changes all of a sudden doesn't mean it's going to stay that way.

❖ Getting distracted is what dawdling is all about, and by the time a child is four or so, toddling and then walking and running have led to the discovery of plenty of distractions in the world beyond themselves. Curiosity about everything is characteristic of that age when a child, as psychologist Margaret Mahler put it, is "engaged in a love affair with the world." Now there's plenty of cause for dawdling, for being distracted by the world. Dawdling becomes so common that grownups even come to expect it, even if they don't appreciate it. Having a wandering mind is part of early childhood and a sign of other things children need to do in addition to getting things done.

✧ I feel quite sure that almost all children have times of uncertainty and jealousy about the newcomer in the family.

✧ The best, I feel, that we can hope is to give children the notion that they can solve the problems that will come to them—that they can have a responsible attitude toward life, toward themselves, and toward others.

✧ It can be fun to be scared, as many of us will recall from Halloweens past. But if we think back, we'll probably agree that there were two things that make it possible for that scariness to be fun. First, we knew that we were safe because someone we loved was nearby. Second, we knew that whatever was scaring us was only pretend.

✧ We often forget what a lot of time we ourselves needed just to figure out how our bodies worked—let alone to begin to understand how all the separate pieces of the world around us fitted together. So often, what babies and toddlers are concentrating on most is the relationship between their bodies and the world.

❖ Certainly, the desire to be like the people they love shapes children's earliest values. A little later, children long to be liked and admired by their friends: to be accepted.

❖ Childhood is not just clowns and balloons. In fact, childhood goes to the very heart of who we all become.

❖ There is a time when things with holes seem particularly fascinating. That's not surprising. The baby's own mouth is an important source of information and comfort in the early weeks and months of life.

❖ When I see a baby quietly staring at his or her own hands . . . or a toddler off in a corner putting something into a cup and then taking it out, over and over again . . . or a preschooler lying in the grass daydreaming, I like to think that they, in their own ways, are "alone in the best room" of their houses, using the solitude they need to find the courage to grow.

❖ There's usually an "inside" story to every "outside" behavior. Though we may not be able to know that "inside story," there's generally some inner reason for what children do.

✧ As children come to be more and more aware of themselves and their world, they also become more aware of how small they are compared with the people who look after them. It may seem that grownups get to do all the big and exciting things and make all the decisions, too. I think it helps children feel good about who they are when we adults put value on the many things children can do. It's a way for us to let them know that we don't want or expect them to be more grownup than they're ready to be—that we really do like them just the way they are.

✧ I remember one time at a personal appearance in Chicago, after singing some songs and showing some puppets, I said to the families in the audience: "Would anybody like to tell me something?" One little boy enthusiastically said, as if he had been waiting all day to tell me, "Mister Rogers, I just wear diapers at night now." And there was a hush over that whole hall as people wondered what in the world I'd make of that little boy's offering. I said, "Well, that's something very important, and it's up to you when you'll give up your diapers at night. I'm really proud of the ways you're growing." The little boy beamed, and there was an audible sigh in the hall.

✧ For young children, comfortable solitude often means being near someone they love.

❖ Knowing that dependence is both available and encouraged when it's needed makes it easier for young children to learn to be healthily independent.

❖ You can see the excitement of growing in children. As a child goes from creeping to standing up and walking, that child usually has very little speech development or other aspects of the toddler's development. It's as though all of that child's energies are bound into that huge task of getting up and walking. It's as if they're obsessed with that one task, and until it's accomplished, they can't concentrate on anything else.

❖ Children who grow up with plenty can learn to give, just as children who grow up receiving love can learn to express it.

❖ A lot of the ways that I feel and a lot of the things that I offer have their roots in the care my early caregivers gave to me.

❖ Even if our childhoods were relatively problem-free, growing always presents us with difficulties to be overcome . . . and the memories of these difficulties are so easily awakened as our children encounter similar difficulties in their own time. It may be a little easier if we know ahead of time that some of the intensity we feel as we try to help our own children with their hard times is very likely related to what we went through ourselves when we were children.

❖ What is important to consider, I think, is the difference between what is imaginary and what is real—and the fears are real.

❖ Moving forward through the early stages of development takes both a push and a pull. The push comes from inside feelings of readiness and confidence. It's a push from within to go on growing. The pull comes from the pleasure a child's caregivers show at signs of growth, and it tugs on every small child's desire to please the people he or she loves.

❖ One thing is certain: Children need lots of free, quiet time to get used to all that's developing within them. Have you noticed that an unhurried time by yourself or with someone you really trust can be the best setting for your own personal growth? It's no different for children.

❖ It is a child's earliest caregivers who lay the groundwork for any child's understanding of "I" and "you" and "we."

✧ Children need adults who are convinced of the value of childhood. They need adults who will protect them from the ever-ready molders of their world. They need adults who can help them to develop their own healthy controls, who can encourage them to explore their own unique endowments, who can know the limits of their ego strengths and not allow programmers of any sort to infringe on those limits. Children need adults—in every walk of life—who care as much for children as they care for themselves.

✧ All life events are formative. All contribute to what we become, year by year, as we go on growing.

✧ What all children need is a secure place in the lives of grown-ups, a place where they can take their own good time to learn that in bringing their growing selves to all the someone elses in this world, they are bringing a gift that is both unique and of value.

✧ In most babies, you can see an awareness of their hands begins when they're about three months old. At first their hands, often clenched into fists, move around in a random way. The fists fly open and clench shut randomly, too. But then there comes a moment when as their hands pass in front of their eyes, the hands stop. It's almost as if the eyes are stopping the hands. When that happens, a new circuit has been completed between eye, mind, and hand. When you think about all we do later on in life, the opening of that circuit becomes a major milestone in our development.

✧ Moving confidently toward independence depends to a great extent on there being a sure foundation of early love to build on, and a fundamental trust that help will be there when we need it. Love and trust are what most enable children to risk trying to be themselves.

✧ I believe that everything in a child's development is connected— what has gone before, what is happening now, and what will happen in the future.

CHAPTER FOUR

Creativity and Play

Pretending you're a pilot or a princess!
Pretending you're a doctor or a king!
Pretending you're a mother or a father.
By pretending you can be
'most anything you want to think about
By pretending.

You can try out life by pretending,
By pretending . . .

—FROM THE SONG "PRETENDING"

❖ What nourishes the imagination? Probably more than anything else, loving adults who encourage the imaginative play of children's own making.

❖ Play is often talked about as if it were a relief from serious learning. But for children, play is serious learning. At various times, play is a way to cope with life and to prepare for adulthood. Playing is a way to solve problems and to express feelings. In fact, play is the real work of childhood.

❖ Art begins within the self. The wellsprings of creativity come from inside.

❖ Grownups are often puzzled by children's play because we don't fully understand, but a child needs the freedom to play what we don't always understand.

❖ Play of a child's own making is a must, because it's how children come to learn so many important things about being human.

✧ When our children show us one of their creations, they are usually trying to tell us something, not create a work of art, and they will get the most encouragement for going on when we show them that we care about what they are trying to say.

✧ There would be no art and there would be no science if human beings had no desire to create. And if we had everything we ever needed or wanted, we would have no reason for creating anything. So, at the root of all art and all science there exists a gap—a gap between what the world is like and what the human creator wishes and hopes for it to be like. Our unique way of bridging that gap in each of our lives seems to me to be the essence of the reason for human creativity.

✧ The way you would draw a tree is different from the way anyone else would draw a tree—and that's the way it's supposed to be!

✧ The urge to make and build seems to be an almost universal human characteristic. It goes way beyond meeting our need for survival and seems to be the expression of some deep-rooted part of being human. It isn't surprising, then, that these acts of creation should be such a large part of children's play.

✧ I have come to realize how important the limits we set for our children are for the development of their creativity: When we won't let them do exactly what they want to do, they have to search out new alternatives.

✧ Early artistic efforts are often attempts to express feelings that may not be able to find their way into words but have to get out somewhere.

✧ Dressing up in grownup clothes can help children to feel big and powerful and in charge of things for a change. Even little children need to feel in control of their world from time to time without the scary responsibility of actually being in control.

✧ Our children take our opinions seriously. What they may need most when they come to show us something they have done (and are so proud of) is a big hug, along with whatever way we have of letting them know, "I really like that, and I'm proud of you for doing it."

✧ Children will spend a lot of time carefully piling blocks up into a tower only to push the building over once it's completed. That often-repeated game seems to be saying, "*I* can build it up, and *I* can knock it down."

✧ Some toys make children conform to them. They are not objects that children could make conform to their own fantasies and feelings. The time spent making those toys work means less time spent in the kind of play that young children need most—play of their own invention. There is a big difference between toys that we can adapt to our inner needs and toys that make us adapt to them.

✧ Early on, I must have been permitted to play on the piano whatever I was feeling. If, instead, my parents had said, "Oh, don't play that loud, ugly stuff, play something pretty and happy," I might have given up "the musical way" of dealing with my feelings.

✧ We want our children to learn to be in control of their actions. If they are to do so, we need to let them control their play as much as they can, so long as their play remains within safe boundaries.

✧ Some grownups may get bothered by the lack of accuracy of a child's drawing. We need to remember, though, that children are not seeking an accurate depiction of outside objects when they draw; they're producing symbols of an inside world. For the most part, what we may consider crude symbols are to them just fine for giving visible expression to what they feel.

✧ There are many reasons why gun play becomes so compelling for our children. That they need to feel powerful and in control is certainly a large part of it.

✧ Guns seem to confer a kind of superpower because they can make things happen at a distance, as though your arms were enormously long. Perhaps for this same reason, remote-control toys have a powerful attraction for young children. Certainly water pistols confer real power. Even flashlights have this power and are reassuring to children who are afraid of the dark.

✧ I don't think many of us believe that when our children play with pretend guns it means that they are likely to grow up to use real ones. But even so, that form of play can be very painful to us because it touches our own deep feelings about death, loss, love, and the value of human life. Those of us who are made uncomfortable by gun play need to let our children know it and let them know in as many ways as we know how that they are very valuable to us.

✧ Just displaying his or her picture on a refrigerator or at the office can make a four-year-old as proud as an artist at a gallery opening.

✧ Just because you're a boy doesn't mean you never had thoughts of wanting to give birth to a baby. Just because you're a girl doesn't mean you never wanted to be a father. Just because you're a grownup doesn't mean you never had thoughts of being a child again. We all have times when we want and need to think of ourselves in unusual ways. It can be a momentary comfort.

✧ I've often hesitated in beginning a project because I've thought, "It'll never turn out to be even remotely like the good idea I have as I start." I could just "feel" how good it *could* be. But I decided that, for the present, I would create the best way I know how and accept the ambiguities.

✧ By offering children appropriate toys to play with, we're letting them know we understand that play is an essential part of their work toward mastery and growth.

✧ Often our puppets on the *Neighborhood* programs allow us to express those parts of our personalities that we might not be quite comfortable expressing all by ourselves. There seems to be a feeling of safety created by the distance between our heads and the puppets on the ends of our hands. That distance allows us to take risks.

❖ One of the most important things a child can learn to do is to make something out of whatever he or she happens to have at the moment.

❖ I often encourage children to wonder about themselves and about the world they're a part of.

❖ Children's dramatic or fantasy play may be as simple as their dressing up and pretending to be other people or as complicated as their construction of a whole little world inhabited by animal and doll figures who go through elaborate rituals and adventures. For many children, dramatic play is one of their most important tools for dealing with everyday problems.

❖ Often the creative urge, once we express it, brings real relief in whatever form its takes. We have an inner sense that we can make what is into what we feel it *could* and *should* be.

✧ Saving children's pictures and putting them up on a wall or a door is one way to give them value, but I don't believe it's helpful always to lavish them with words like "wonderful" and "beautiful." Extravagant praise of that kind can lead children to have unrealistic expectations for themselves, expectations that, in turn, can lead to later disappointments.

✧ We can keep the difference between reality and fantasy as clear as we can by encouraging our children to engage in make-believe play as much as they want to, but by reinforcing, at the same time, that some things are only pretend.

✧ I think that a large part of children's making and building play comes from the desire to feel in control of the outside world and the inner self. When children play with blocks, they are making the decision about what form the blocks will take and what they will represent. A child simply makes what he or she feels the need to make. In doing so, the child is in control of what takes place. Being able to express his or her feelings through making and creating is a healthy part of a child's growing.

✧ When children play with puppets, the distance is comfortable enough so that what they might not have wanted to say themselves, they can say through the puppets.

❖ Often parents find that at a certain age young children turn almost everything they pick up into a "gun," and if there isn't anything to pick up, a cocked thumb and forefinger will do just as well.

❖ Playing about war is very different from having a real war. Play is one of the important ways children can work through their concerns. Of course, war play can become scary or unsafe. At times like that, children need to know adults are nearby to help reassure them, to stop the play when it becomes too scary, and to redirect the play into caring and nurturing themes, perhaps by suggesting they build a hospital for people who are hurt or tents and homes where others could go to eat and sleep.

❖ Creativity and imagination are the beginning of problem-solving for a young child.

❖ "Here's the kind of world I expect you to build." That's the implicit message children may get from the playthings we offer them. What serious business that makes for both our children and ourselves.

❖ There are all kinds of artists in the world. If people can combine the talent that they have inside of them with the hard work that it takes to develop it, they can become a true artist of some kind.

❖ If we ask them, our children are often willing to tell us what their pictures mean to them, and we, in return, can tell our children how their pictures make us feel. If the artwork our children create does result in such moments of closeness and sharing, then our children are likely to want to do more.

❖ Through play, children can use puppets or doll figures or art materials to express their feelings of anger and sadness at what hurts and who hurts; and they can do it without risking the loss of love that just might be the result of acted-out anger.

❖ Many children have imaginary friends. I think that's because when a young child wishes for something that he or she doesn't have, that child will often create it by imagining it. That's a normal part of childhood.

❖ We can often guess what's bothering children when they allow us to watch their play when they're drawing or pretending or making up stories. And we can encourage them to go on playing about their feelings, too. The more they can handle scary things in their play, the less scary such things need to seem everywhere else.

❖ It takes a lot of growing for children to feel secure about what's real and what's pretend. We need to encourage our children in their play, but we need to remember that the normal fears and fantasies of early childhood, even when acted out in pretending, are very real indeed.

❖ One way to think about play is as the process of finding new combinations for known things—combinations that may yield new forms of expression, new inventions, new discoveries, and new solutions. I like thinking about play in this way because it gives play some of the importance it deserves.

❖ There have always been times when children wished for superhuman powers. Cave children probably pretended to be superhunters, just as children today pretend about being superstrong or superfast.

❧ Parents can help greatly in creating a sense of safety for their children's play. They can give their children safe places to play and safe toys to play with. They can help their children learn the difference between real and pretend. They can let their children know that their play is their own, to make of it what they will.

❧ Play allows us a safe distance as we work on what's close to our hearts.

❧ Imagining something may be the first step in making it happen, but it takes the real time and real efforts of real people to learn things, make things, turn thoughts into deeds or visions into inventions.

❧ I'm often asked if I think there's something about electronic games that is actually bad for children. What I have come to believe is this: The healthiest playthings for young children are those that a child can make conform to his or her own unique fantasies and feelings. By and large, electronic games do just the opposite. They make a child conform to the program inside the machine. It may be true that electronic games can increase a child's eye-hand coordination and even some kinds of concentration. I'd like to think that's so. Where I become concerned, however, is when I see electronic games becoming the mainstay of a child's play.

❖ Showing an active interest in what a child is doing is sometimes the best compliment of all.

❖ Pretending doesn't require expensive toys.

❖ Children's play can become obsessive, like when they throw things down from their high chairs over and over, expecting parents to retrieve them again and again. It's only natural that parents can get impatient and irritated after a while. It can help to understand that their children's obsessions express some kind of need. At the same time, children need to learn that there are appropriate when's, where's, and how-to's for giving expression to their feelings. It can often be helpful for parents to set aside particular times for allowing and supporting obsessive play of one kind or another—whether it's throwing and retrieving, smearing and making messes, or pretending to have an imaginary family.

❖ Children, of course, grow up with different models of authority in their families, and it's likely to be these (at least those that seem to work) that they first try out in their play. But other children have other models, so even in preschool the clashes and negotiations of "office politics" begin.

❧ What I have heard from creative people over the years is that their early urges toward unique self-expression were respected and supported by some loving adult in their young lives—someone who would even let them paint a tree blue if that's what they felt like doing. When a friend of mine was a little boy, he liked to draw and paint a lot. One time he drew a tree and colored it blue, and some grownup said to him, "Why did you color a tree blue? Trees aren't blue!" My friend didn't draw a tree again for years . . . not until one of his teachers told him that artists can make things any shape and any color they want.

❧ In order to be an inventor, you have to be able to imagine something first . . . before you can make it.

❧ When people help us to feel good about who we are, they are really helping us love the meaning of what we create in this life.

❧ From what I read and hear and see, I have no doubt that millions of children of all ages are getting an overdose of mechanical entertainment and suffering a deficiency in healthier forms of play. Although I don't know what the consequences will be, I feel sure they will be measurable and specific and will affect the quality of human relationships and the individual's capacity for self-development.

❧ Every child is born with a unique endowment that gives him an opportunity to make something entirely different from everybody else in the world. You see it when you watch children at their own play. There are no two mud pies the same.

❧ Block buildings have infinite variety. Paintings and dances take on their creators' touches and later, hairstyles, jewelry, and language; and when you see it all happening, you know that something from inside is being shared with the rest of the world.

❧ Creativity is a strong and natural part of early childhood. It may even be inborn and something infants rely on as they try to understand the workings of this world. Finding your thumb and bringing yourself comfort for a while is, for many children, one of the earliest experiences of creativity.

❧ People whose work is creative self-expression of the most obvious kind—artists, writers, musicians, dancers—seem to be drawing heavily on play to do what they do. What they all have in common is the urge to take what is known and rearrange it in new combinations.

❧ It's not easy to come up with a definition of play that feels just right. And that's probably because something deep within all of us "knows" the immense value of play.

❧ Without human beings there never would have been a computer or anything else that we call advanced technology. That's something I like to help children remember: that, no matter what the machine may be, it was *people* who thought it up and made it, and it's people who make it work.

❧ It's the things we play with and the people who help us play that make a great difference in our lives.

❧ As we offer playthings that are tools of healthy problem-solving, not weapons, to our children, we'll be giving them an attitude toward conflict that can ensure a much richer, longer life for them and the planet we all call home.

❧ What happens if children hear that their mud pies are no good and their block buildings have no importance, that their paintings and dances and made-up games and songs are of very little value? What do you think happens to that something from inside—that self that was trying itself on the world for size? What do you think?

✧ In order to express our sense of reality, we must use some kind of symbol: words or notes or shades of paint or television pictures or sculpted forms. None of those symbols or images can ever completely satisfy us because they can never be any more than what they are—a fragment of a reflection of what we feel reality to be.

✧ Being creative is part of being human. Everyone is creative. Each person's creativity finds different form, that's true; but without creativity of some kind, I doubt that we'd get through many of the problems that life poses. It's certainly one of the most important coping skills that parents can help their children develop.

✧ Play is an expression of our creativity, and creativity, I believe, is at the very root of our ability to learn, to cope, and to become whatever we may be.

CHAPTER FIVE

Discipline

Sometimes people are good,
And they do just what they should.

But the very same people who are good
      sometimes
Are the very same people who are bad
      sometimes.
It's funny but it's true.
It's the same, isn't it, for me and you . . .

    —FROM THE SONG
      "SOMETIMES PEOPLE ARE GOOD"

❖ We feed our children, and as we do so, we help them feed themselves. We keep them clean and warm, and we try to keep them healthy, until they learn to do those things for themselves, too. And in the same way, we provide our children with the discipline they need until they learn to exercise it for themselves.

❖ When we give a young child choices, we acknowledge that child's individuality. And when a child's urge to be an individual gets channeled into choice-making, it's less likely to go into contrariness.

❖ That chores have to be done before play; that patient persistence is often the only road to mastery; that anger can be expressed through words and nondestructive activities; that promises are intended to be kept; that cleanliness and good eating habits are aspects of self-esteem; that compassion is an attribute to be prized—all these are lessons children can learn far more readily through the living example of their parents than they ever can through formal instruction.

❧ It's so easy to say "Bad boy!" or "Bad girl!" to a child who spills or breaks or hits or bites or gets dirty. But the child is likely to hear "I am bad" rather than "What I did was bad," and a child who feels he or she is a bad person is also likely to feel unlovable. If we come to believe that we are unlovable, there's likely to be little motivation to avoid doing bad things.

❧ Disciplining a child—that is, lending them our controls while they need it—is a loving gift and can be one of the great satisfactions of parenting.

❧ Children, when they're young, need a lot of limits. Many are for their health and safety, such as what can be touched and what cannot, what is good to eat and what is not, where it's safe to play and where it's not. Other limits are set to help children move comfortably among other people—what they can say to whom, what they can do and where. Happy and healthy family life depends on limits, some that keep family life moving on schedule, others that serve to protect privacy and property.

❧ While children do need permission to feel their feelings, they often need limits on the expression of them.

❖ Call them rules or call them limits, good ones have this in common: They serve reasonable purposes; they are practical and within a child's capability; they are consistent; and they are an expression of loving concern.

❖ Parents of toddlers have to become very careful of what's around. It seems obvious to most parents to keep dangerous things away from those hungry hands, but it's easy to overlook the importance of feeding those hands with things that are not only safe but also varied and interesting in shape and texture. This hunger of the hands is an urgent outreach to the world. It's one of the earliest forms of curiosity and exploration, of discovery and pleasure. It's also a beginning of very important learning—the meaning of the word "no" and the importance of self-control.

❖ Often, a parent will find it easier to maintain a safe limit for a child in a firm but loving way if she can let her child make reasonable decisions about other parts of his or her life.

❖ Destroying our own block buildings, pounding our own clay creations, scribbling over our own drawings—all these aggressive acts can vent anger in permissible ways.

✧ One of the worst feelings is the feeling of being out of control, and one of the most helpful things we can do is to discover ways of encouraging children to be in control.

✧ The appropriateness of a punishment depends on the unique personality and experiences of each individual parent and each child, and, above all, on the unique quality of the relationship between them.

✧ Disciplining a child includes making rules. I prefer to think of this parenting task as "setting limits."

✧ Often, the way we choose to punish our children reflects the way we were punished by our parents. Characteristics of parenting do tend to carry over from generation to generation. Punishment, too, has a lot to do with cultural traditions and values—as do the decisions concerning what kinds of actions require punishment.

✧ It can be very frightening for a child not to have limits. Not only can the world outside be frightening, but the world inside, the world of feelings, can also be scary when you're not sure you can manage those feelings by yourself.

✧ There are times, of course, when all parents have to set limits on dawdling. Those limits, though, need to be set and explained with care so that children don't come to feel that we're trying to restrict their limitless capacity to fall in love with life.

✧ Providing a framework doesn't take away children's individuality. In fact, structure generally helps them to be more free because it provides boundaries. It's like a fence that offers security for what can happen inside the enclosure. Respect flourishes best within a clear framework, and it's that framework that can allow us all to express more of who we really are.

✧ Children may sometimes find our reasons for rules hard to understand or may consider the rules unreasonable. "But Janie's parents let her stay up until ten" is something we may hear. I think the answer's a simple one that children in their own way can comprehend. "But you're not growing up in Janie's family, and we feel different about it."

✧ While children certainly need to learn about limits and consequences, they also need the staunch support of grownups who help them believe in their capacity to make it through.

❖ No child is born with self-discipline.

❖ Often, our quiet availability is just what children need, far more than they need our coaxes or cajolings or threats or punishments. Our reassuring presence may be enough to help them find inner resources of their own, and when they do, parents and children can both feel proud.

❖ Discipline and punishment are different. I think of discipline as the continuous everyday process of helping a child learn self-discipline.

❖ It's a rare parent who hasn't lost his or her temper and reacted verbally or physically. No one, even an adult, is in control all the time. Young children can learn a lot from us when, after the heat of the moment has passed, we can apologize for something we did that was inappropriate. It's good discipline (for us, as well as for our children) to be able to say, "I'm sorry I got angry, and I shouldn't have hit you. I was really scared you were going to get hurt. But you do have to learn not to touch sharp knives because you could get cut."

❖ "Sometimes People Are Good" and "Good People Sometimes Do Bad Things" are songs I sing to let children know that everyone does things that are naughty once in a while but that doing something bad doesn't make you a bad person.

❖ I believe that children welcome our efforts to control any behavior that might hurt others. One of the things they may have to understand from our limit-setting is that we won't let other people hurt them, either.

❖ Angry words are a healthier outlet for feelings of rage and aggression than are angry acts such as hitting, kicking, or biting. Those are the outlets that come naturally to toddlers who haven't much language to use. Learning to replace these actions with words instead is, in fact, a sign of healthy growth.

❖ There's a reason for every behavior. When children are uncooperative and noncommunicative, that may be their only way of being in control of something.

❖ Disciplining a child includes comfort, care, and nurture, passing on traditions and values, and praise for achievement; and it most certainly includes examples, from which young children learn so much.

❧ Discipline depends less on distance and authority than it does on intimacy and trust.

❧ Setting limits for their children is one of the most important ways parents can regulate their children's behavior . . . and help them become self-regulating adults.

❧ There's a world of difference between insisting on someone's doing something and establishing an atmosphere in which that person can grow into wanting to do it.

❧ When I asked one of my colleagues, "What is discipline?" she replied: "Discipline is the gift of responsible love." I think it's hard to improve on that description.

❧ Controls of any kind can be hard to achieve. What seems to help parents most is trying to distinguish between what is possible for their children and what isn't—and then giving their children the caring support all children need until they learn to use the controls for themselves.

❧ It is not an easy thing for children in groups to control their impulses. What helps them feel comfortable is knowing there are adults in charge who will take charge by providing the control they need.

❧ Children feel safer when they know what the rules are.

❧ There are many times, as children grow, when they need to borrow from a grownup's self-control, and knowing they can do so helps them develop greater self-control of their own. In the security of a parent's presence, children can often find the strength to regain the mastery of their feelings that they were about to lose . . . and once again feel ready to go on coping.

❧ It can be one of parents' most difficult jobs to walk the fine line between giving in to their children's whims and punishing them for what are basically healthy attempts to discover who they are.

❧ Often, refusing to go along with old ways and familiar limits is the best thing a young child can do to try out new feelings of being a separate individual.

❦ If you don't love yourself or the people who care for you, why should you bother to give up the breast or the bottle, or give up soiling your pants, or for that matter why should you adapt yourself to any of the ways of society . . . if you don't have anybody to please?

❦ Bathroom words are often a child's first swear words, and there's a natural reason for that. Children are rapidly acquiring language at the same time that they're moving through toilet training. Once they're clean and dry (more or less), they quickly learn that an almost sure way to make a parent unhappy or even angry is to have an "accident." They still want to please the people they love, and so they're usually unwilling to have accidents on purpose. Odd as it may seem, this kind of language is a way of turning the accident into words . . . and that's growth.

❦ It's important to say "I'm proud of you" if we see a child ready to hit who finds control and holds back.

❦ Expecting children to make a sudden switch to bedtime from the stimulation of roughhousing or television is asking more than most of them can give.

❖ Because of food's deeper meanings, I believe it's worth a lot of patience, understanding, and self-control on the part of parents to avoid turning mealtimes into battlegrounds. I'm not even comfortable when mealtimes become bargaining sessions.

❖ Toddlers' hands seem to have an appetite that just can't be satisfied! When we caution them or forbid them to reach out and touch certain things, they may be able to restrain themselves so long as we're right there, close by. Their own self-control is just beginning to grow, though, and as soon as our backs are turned, they may seem to "disobey." It's not disobeying, however, and there's nothing stubborn or willful or bad about the insistent hunger of their hands.

❖ We all have negative urges, but we don't have to act out those urges.

✧ Love, I feel quite certain, is at the root of all healthy discipline. The desire to be loved is a powerful motivation for children to behave in ways that give their parents pleasure rather than displeasure. It may even be our own long-ago fear of losing our parents' love that now sometimes makes us uneasy about setting and maintaining limits. We're afraid we'll lose the love of our children when we don't let them have their way. So we parents need to try to find the security within ourselves to accept the fact that we and our children won't always like one another's actions, that there will be times when we and our children won't be able to be "friends," and that there will be times of real anger within the family.

CHAPTER SIX

Learning

If you want to read a reading book
And read the real words, too,
You can't simply sit and ask
The words to read themselves to you.
But you have to ask a person
Who can show you one or two
If you want to read a reading book
And read the real words, too.

It's not easy to keep trying,
But it's one good way to grow.
It's not easy to keep learning,
But I know that this is so:
When you've tried and learned
You're bigger than you were a day ago.
It's not easy to keep trying,
But it's one way to grow.

—FROM THE SONG
"YOU'VE GOT TO DO IT"

❦ Learning and loving go hand in hand. My grandfather was one of those people who loved to live and loved to teach. Every time I was with him, he'd show me something about the world or something about myself that I hadn't even thought of yet. He'd help me find something wonderful in the smallest of things, and ever so carefully, he helped me understand the enormous worth of every human being. My grandfather was not a professional teacher, but the way he treated me (the way he *loved* me) and the things he did with me served me as well as any teacher I've ever known.

❦ As far as I'm concerned, this is the essence of education: to facilitate a person's learning, to help that person become more in tune with his or her own resources so that he or she can use whatever is offered more fully.

❦ Nobody learns unless he or she is ready to learn.

❦ What are the basic necessities for children to be ready to learn? (1) a sense of self-worth, (2) a sense of trust, (3) curiosity, (4) the capacity to look and listen carefully, (5) the capacity to play, and (6) times of solitude.

✧ One of the hardest things for young children to understand is that their actions have real consequences for others. That's because for a time a child's own world seems like the whole world: That's all there is.

✧ Children are people, and they must take their time—inner time that is common to all—to develop normally. When we ask a child to read before he has developed the ability to abstract, we ask that child to do something he cannot do. When his inner rhythm tells him he's ready (and willing), *he'll learn*—just the way he learned to crawl by following his insistent developmental need.

✧ As children grow, it's important that they are able to love the person who they are, so they will continue to want to learn and succeed in life.

✧ "Attitudes are caught, not taught." That's a wise Quaker saying. When I was doing my practicum work in child development at the University of Pittsburgh, I remember hearing about a gifted sculptor who was a father of a kindergartner. At the request of the director, this man came to the kindergarten once a week and simply loved clay in the midst of the children. He didn't *teach* about clay, he just loved it and fashioned it and showed how he could express his feelings with it in that place where the children could watch him. And little by little, the children themselves began to *love* their clay and what it felt like to work with it and what they found they could make of it. That sculpting father came regularly for a whole year! I'm told that not before or since in that kindergarten have children used the medium of clay in such imaginative, satisfying ways—all because they caught the enthusiasm of someone who loved what he did right in front of them!

✧ Children are not merely vessels into which facts are poured one week and then when it comes time for exams they turn themselves upside down and let the facts run out. Children bring all of themselves, their feelings, and their experiences to the learning.

✧ I think that a fear of the world has a lot to do with some children's difficulty in looking carefully and listening carefully. I'm thinking of those children who grow up amidst deprivation and in surroundings where so much of what there is to look at and listen to is painful and scary. A human being can take only so much frightening stimulation, and then he or she is likely to shut off the desire to look at or listen to anything carefully. If a child is confronted with murder, rape, domestic violence, and other kinds of destructive aggression in daily life, it doesn't surprise me if that child "turns off" careful looking and listening. I even feel that this may be one of the most frequent causes of trouble for children who can't learn to read.

❧ There's a lot of talk these days about "education" and what children need for learning. Before narrowing learning down to three black marks, like *C A T* on a piece of paper, I would rather see a child be in the presence of someone who cares about children and about cats, someone who can help him or her come to respect cats for their grace and independence, grow to know that cats have feelings, that they need food and water, that each one is different, that they get tired and they sleep and they need to be loved.

❧ I don't believe any educational gimmicks can be very helpful in teaching children who are burdened with overwhelming anxieties. For them, learning readiness really means the reestablishment of trust.

❧ No matter how helpful computers are as tools in the classroom (and of course, they can be very helpful tools), they don't begin to compare in significance to the relationship between the teacher and the child that is human and mutual.

❧ A computer can help you learn to spell *hug*, but it can never help you know the risk or the joy of actually giving or receiving one.

❧ Knowing that we're valued and being in the presence of people who want to share with us something of this world that they love are the two most important ingredients of education.

❧ An unhurried morning routine at home can help your child get ready—and feel ready—for school without haste or anxiety. Sending him or her off with a cheerful "Have a good day in school!" or "See you after school!" is much more encouraging than an admonition like "Be good!"

❧ A berry ripens in its own good time . . . and so does a child's readiness. Just as the one needs water and sunlight, the other needs the patient reassurance of loving adults who can trust children to grow according to their own timetables.

❧ It may be that the most important mastery a child achieves early on is not the mastery of a particular skill or a particular piece of knowledge, but rather the mastery of the patience and persistence that learning requires, along with the ability to expect and accept mistakes and the feelings of disappointment they may bring.

❖ Learning to look and listen carefully is an important part of "learning to learn." I believe that children are born with the ability to concentrate, but often something seems to interrupt the development of that ability.

❖ School systems work on a fixed schedule, and human development doesn't.

❖ Sustained attention to things tends to foster deliberate thought. Readiness to develop the capacity for deliberate thought begins very early as children engage in their own kind of thinking—daydreaming, fantasizing, and making up all kinds of activities that we call play.

❖ A love of learning has a lot to do with learning that we're loved.

❖ I believe that the basis of any health education lies in a person's caring enough about himself that he'll want to take care of himself. If we want people to eat the right food, brush their teeth, get the proper exercise, seek regular checkups, avoid cigarettes, dope, and poison, we must help these people feel that they're really *worth* taking care of.

✣ Play gives children a chance to practice what they are learning.

✣ Children who are about a year old may spend a lot of time practicing about the inside and outside of things . . . over and over putting a block in a box and taking it out again. How else except through this kind of play is a child to understand the difference between the inside and outside of things?

✣ What matters even more than superimposing adult symbols is how a person's inner life finally puts together the alphabet and numbers of his outer life. What really matters is whether he uses the alphabet for the declaration of a war or the description of a sunrise, his numbers for the final count at Buchenwald or the specifics of a brand-new bridge.

✣ "Why can't my boy concentrate?" might be rephrased "Where can my boy concentrate?" Perhaps we could find a missing link in a child's development that way.

To grow up to be healthy, very young children do not need to know how to read, but they need to know how to play. Lest you wonder if I'm against reading and books, I must tell you that I would much rather spend an evening reading a book than doing almost anything else. But there's a world of difference between insisting on someone's doing something and establishing an atmosphere in which that person can grow into wanting to do it!

CHAPTER SEVEN

Difficult
Situations

I like to be told
When you're going away,
When you're going to come back,
And how long you will stay.

I like to be told
If it's going to hurt,
If it's going to be hard,
If it's not going to hurt.
I like to be told.

It helps me to get ready for all those things,
All those things that are new.
I trust you more and more each time
That I'm finding those things to be true . . .

—FROM THE SONG "I LIKE TO BE TOLD"

✧ For a child, moving through life within a family may be a little like being in an airplane: There may be a lot of rough weather outside, and the plane may shake around quite a bit, but inside you're safe. Sad, scared, and angry, perhaps, but within the special atmosphere of a loving family, even those feelings are safe. When a child learns to trust that there is a loving caregiver right there to help in rough times, he or she can weather most any storm—and ultimately be stronger for the experience.

✧ Children need adults who realize that losses to children are every bit as painful as losses to adults.

✧ Feelings are mentionable, and whatever is mentionable can be more manageable. Whether we're children or adults, adding to our emotional vocabulary can often add to our ability to cope with what we're feeling. Using words to describe what's inside helps remind us that what we're experiencing is human . . . and mentioning our feelings to others can make those feelings more manageable.

✧ It's always remarkable to me that children can find their way through complex and turbulent emotions, bring them to healthy resolutions, and turn out capable of forming loving and lasting relationships of their own.

❖ Moving, divorce, and death are, of course, very different kinds of experiences from one another; but whether it's a home, a family structure, or a loved person, the loss is real, the grief can be profound, and it may include a good deal of anger at having had something taken away, as well as sadness that it's gone.

❖ Young children don't know that sadness isn't forever. It's frightening for them to feel that their sadness may overwhelm them and never go away. "The very same people who are sad sometimes are the very same people who are glad sometimes" is something all parents need to help their children come to understand.

❖ How we deal with the big disappointments in life depends a great deal on how the people who loved us helped us deal with smaller disappointments when we were little.

❖ Love makes all losses possible—makes the ego able to accept them.

❖ Many of us who work with children have seen how helpful it is to them to talk and play about the feelings they have from the crises they've been through. It seems that children's strong feelings naturally tend to show up in their play, but it certainly helps if their close caregivers support such play by letting them know it's not only okay, but important. If we can learn to talk and play about our feelings when we're young, we may be able to take that capacity with us through life. It could make the difference, when strong winds hit us, between bending and breaking.

❧ Often, problems are knots with many strands, and looking at those strands can make a problem seem different.

❧ One mother with a child who had been terribly frightened all of the time told us, "I've come to understand that, like everyone else, Nathan needs acceptance, understanding, tolerance, patience, and love—and then he does have the resources for dealing with life."

❧ We parents are often surprised to find how readily our young children offer us comfort at times of honest talk about our feelings. Children need to feel needed just as much as the rest of us do!

❧ Many children who go through significant changes in their lives experience a loss of competence. And if the child isn't made to feel foolish for that normal setback, that child will gain back the losses and be able to grow beyond them.

✧ We'd all like to feel self-reliant and capable of coping with whatever adversity comes our way, but that's not how most human beings are made. It's my belief that the capacity to accept help is inseparable from the capacity to give help when our turn comes to be strong.

✧ Children who are encouraged in their own unique forms of artwork can come to use them as very reliable aids for understanding and coping with the stresses that accompany all their growing. The more serious the stresses, the more people need to be able to call on such a resource within themselves.

✧ We need time to miss the people and the things we lose (no matter whether the loss is temporary or permanent).

✧ "The amazing thing I've seen in my children," one unemployed father told us, "is that they do grasp the concept of Daddy being out of work. Yet they are so optimistic and encouraging. It helps us go on." That father identifies one of the priceless opportunities of parenthood: the ability to borrow from our children's strength, even as we lend them ours.

✧ What are the most painful things to lose? For most of us, I believe, they're things that represent people—a family heirloom, a grandparent's diary, a piece of embroidery made by a parent, a scarf that a friend always wore. When things like that get lost, we may feel as though a part of ourselves has gone because those people were part of who we are. Any time we feel that we've lost a part of ourselves, we can be sure it's going to hurt . . . really hurt.

✧ How often the truth has been borne out that when a child is confronted by something that's frustrating or difficult and is able to come to terms with it, using a combination of his own resources and the resources of the adults around him, not only is he or she able to grow through the difficulty but grow in greater strength than ever before.

✧ Grandparents can be very special resources. Just being close to them reassures a child, without words, about change and continuity, about what went before and what will come after.

✧ Children's fantasies about what might happen to them are often so much more frightening than what the reality is.

✧ Sometimes adults feel that immediate restitution is best after there's been a loss. But unless a child is given time to grieve, to cry and play out the significant losses of childhood, the consequences could continue for a lifetime.

✧ There are times when explanations, no matter how reasonable, just don't seem to help.

✧ Some of my richest experiences have come out of the most painful times . . . those that were the hardest to believe would ever turn into anything positive.

✧ When there is pain or sorrow in our children's lives, as there is bound to be, there is often no way we can make it go away. Nevertheless, when children can cope with hard times—drawing on whatever comfort they find from us and from themselves—their parents can be very proud indeed. That ability to cope may be one of the greatest abilities that parents can help their children acquire.

✧ At many times throughout their lives, children will feel the world has turned topsy-turvy. It's not the ever-present smile that will help them feel secure. It's knowing that love can hold many feelings, including sadness, and that they can count on the people they love to be with them until the world turns right side up again.

✧ One challenge to parents is how to raise loving, trusting children while at the same time instilling a sense of healthy wariness of strangers.

✧ Our children will learn a lot about expressing their feelings by watching how we express ours. And we need to let them know that the violent expressions of anger that they see around them are not the way it has to be. Above all, we need to try to show our children that we love and value them. By doing so, we can help them learn that there is much in the world to love and value as well . . . and that goes for the people in it, too.

✧ I don't believe that children, when they're very young, need to be told about all the troubles in this world. In fact, they may need our reassurance that the world isn't really as sad or dangerous or scary a place as it may seem in the pictures of it that come to them through media such as television.

✧ When I was a child and would see scary things on the news, my mother would say to me, "Look for the helpers. You will always find people who are helping."

✧ There are no perfect parents, and there are no perfect children. But imperfect parents can be loving parents, and the gifts of their love can be enough to preserve "the child within" from despair when times get rough.

✧ There's never been a time in our history when there have been so many changes, so many unusual things to deal with for which we have no experience. It's as if our whole society were walking along a road through a wilderness of constant change with strangers we think we should know, but don't quite understand.

✧ I heard a song the other day. It started with these words: "Whatever happened to old-fashioned love? The kind that would see you through? The kind that my mama and daddy knew?" and I thought of the longing that all of us have for some comfort and stability—something to hold on to in these rapidly changing times.

✧ I believe that for many violent adults the start of it all lies in the earliest years of their lives. We all have angry and even violent feelings within us, but most of us learn, as we grow, how to express those feelings in ways that don't hurt either others or ourselves.

✧ The impact of television must be considered in the light of the possibility that children are exposed to experiences that may be far beyond what their egos can deal with effectively.

✧ I feel that one reason there is such an outcry against violence and sex on the screen is that they are both so often represented *out* of human context. A Sunday *New York Times* article by William Gale included interviews with members of some South Bronx street gangs. These young people have some striking opinions about television. Karate Charlie Suarez believes television glamorizes violence. People, he says, aren't just naturally disposed toward violence. They've got to be helped along. And he feels TV violence is a big culprit. "Bang, bang, you're dead. That's all. They show just the violence. No real pain. No funeral. No plot of earth. No sign of what happens to the wife and kids after that guy gets killed." I think that's a very sensitive statement by a young man who has already seen many of the consequences of violence.

✧ In any time of family, community, or worldwide stress, the most important question in a young child's mind is "Who will take care of me?" Young children can't take care of themselves, so in order to survive, they must have others to take care of them. The best we adults can do is to let our children know that we'll take good care of them—no matter what. That's what helps them grow—in good times and in bad.

✧ Much of television is degrading. What parents give their children, though, will always be more important than what television gives them. Children who are loved and feel they are lovable are the ones who are most likely to grow into loving, rather than violent, adults. Taking the time to help our children understand their world and their place in it, as well as what they see on television, is a way of letting our children know they are unique, valuable human beings who can learn to express their own aggressive feelings in healthy, nonviolent ways.

✧ If we haven't thought about it before, we're very likely to be taken aback by our children's first questions about death.

✧ Thinking about death seems to be parents' necessary first step in finding words for their children.

✧ I've sometimes said to a child who has had a loved one die, "It can make a person mad to have someone go away and not come back, can't it?" I've had children nod in reply as if to say, "Yes, that's what I'm feeling." Then I might say something like "Well, a lot of people feel mad when someone they love dies." Just identifying a feeling and hearing that there's nothing wrong with it seems to be a big help to a child and to make it possible for him or her to talk more about it—then or later.

✧ I remember, after my grandfather's death, seeing Dad in the hall with tears streaming down his face. I don't think I had ever seen him cry before. I'm glad I did see him. It helped me know that it was okay for men to cry. Many years later, when my father himself died, I cried; and way down deep I knew he would have said it was all right.

✧ Death is the subject of many misunderstandings, perhaps because adults often have a hard time talking about it simply and directly. Saying that "Grammy went to sleep and never woke up" may seem like a gentle way to break the news of a close relative's death, but it has led to nighttime fears for many children who begin worrying that if they let themselves go to sleep, they may never wake up either.

✧ We need to be honest with our children, saying that we don't know when we don't . . . and that we sometimes wonder about death, too.

✧ It can be hard to know just what children need from us when there has been a death of a loved one, but very often the same things that can help us can help them, too—simple things like hugging, talking, being close, and having quiet times together.

✧ Divorces don't wreck children's lives. People do.

✧ Motherly love and fatherly love do not cease when the love between husband and wife ends and turns to anger. It's up to mothers and fathers to let their children know that; but in order to do so, they have to know it themselves—know it so fully and deeply that their parental love is expressed in acts and not just words.

✧ Forgiveness is as important to our emotional well-being as being able to wait for what we want or to cope with stress. Like most of the important inner strengths of life, the ability to forgive (to let go of resentments, to give up being an accuser) takes root early in our becoming.

❖ Children need to know divorce is a grownup problem. When tragic things happen in a family, children naturally think it's because of something they did. It's important that they hear that it's not their fault.

❖ Parents often worry about how their young children are going to weather a move. One important suggestion is to acknowledge the feelings of loss everyone is likely to feel. It's rare for a family to move without suffering at least some pangs over leaving people and places that have grown familiar. For many families, these feelings are very deep and painful.

❖ Children don't understand medical procedures and why they have to go through so much pain and frustration. Even though people tell them a hundred times that the hurtful treatments are going to help them get better, they're still angry, and one of their desperate needs is to have some socially acceptable way of communicating and expressing their anger.

❖ Most children who are ill or have some kind of disability are afraid of their angry wishes. Their parents are afraid of their own anger, too. They're afraid that any anger in themselves and in any others around them might end up in death.

❖ For sick children, a caring person is even more important than for other children, because so much that happens to the sick child tends to foster regression in order for that child to feel safe. That caring person helps the child keep his or her sense of self intact, so the child doesn't need to regress so far backward.

❖ Being in the best hospital in the world is still second-best to being home . . . and well.

CHAPTER EIGHT

Communicating

What if I were very, very sad
And all I did was smile?
I wonder after a while
What might become of my sadness?

What if I were very, very angry
And all I did was sit
And never think about it?
What might become of my anger?

Where would they go, and what would
      they do,
If I couldn't let them out?
Maybe I'd fall, maybe get sick
Or doubt.

But what if I could know the truth
And say just how I feel?
I think I'd learn a lot that's real
About freedom . . .

    —FROM THE SONG
      "THE TRUTH WILL MAKE ME FREE"

✧ Listening is where love begins: listening to ourselves and then to our neighbors.

✧ Find the simplest truthful answers.

✧ Bill Bixby, who was an actor and a caring father, told me how he talked with his own son about the pretending on television. He said something to me of real value. As he put it: "If you don't talk, you don't touch."

✧ The older I get, the more convinced I am that the space between communicating human beings can be hallowed ground.

✧ It's understandable that we and our children find many things hard to talk about. But anything that's human is mentionable, and anything that's mentionable can be more manageable. Don't you often find that just having a good listener makes your upsetting times more manageable? When we can talk about our feelings, they can become less overwhelming, less upsetting, and less scary. The people we trust with that important talk can help us know that we're not alone and that our feelings are natural and normal.

✧ Confronting our feelings and giving them the appropriate expression always takes strength, not weakness.

✧ More and more I have come to understand that listening is one of the most important things we can do for one another. Whether the other is an adult or a child, our engagement in listening to who that person is can often be our greatest gift to that person. Whether that person is speaking or playing or dancing, building or singing or painting, if we care, we can do our best to listen.

✧ How essential it is to find safe ways of expressing how we feel about what is important to us!

✧ When we're trying to tell a child something that's very important and that child just can't seem to understand, it could be helpful for us to listen with the child's ear, with the child's words. As we do, we adults will be learning more about who we are, and in the best possible sense, we'll be watching our tongues.

✧ We speak with more than our mouths. We listen with more than our ears.

✧ Children have many ways to let us know that something upsets them. For example, they might let us know through changes in their sleeping or eating habits, or by being more dependent or demanding.

✧ Young children sometimes look sheepish when they confide in us, as though they already suspect there's something amiss in their interpretation of the world; and have you noticed how often older children, even teenagers, will start a confidence with a question like "Promise you won't laugh if I tell you?"

✧ Listening and trying to understand the needs of those we would communicate with seems to me to be the essential prerequisite of any real communication. And we might as well aim for *real* communication.

✧ The greatest gift you ever give is your honest self.

❦ No matter what our children ask us, we can always say, "I'm not quite sure how to explain that right now, but we'll talk about it later." That's a promise that needs to be kept, but as a response to questions about touchy subjects, it's often the simplest truth of all.

❦ Children can carry feelings for a very long time if they don't have an opportunity to talk with someone about them. And when they are able to trust and share, they often feel freed to be more communicative in a variety of ways.

❦ The end of the school day is usually an exciting time for a child and a time when he or she needs you to listen to what went on—what was fun, what wasn't, what was easy, what the other children did, what the teacher said. Taking a little time to really listen can both give you insights into how things are going at school and give your child the sense that you care about his or her life at school and that you are proud of the ways he or she is learning and growing.

❦ There is a close relationship between truth and trust.

❦ I don't believe there's any such thing as a meaningless communication between caregiver and child—not from the first touch or coo. Each, no matter how seemingly insignificant, adds to the stored experiences of all messages that have gone before. All this stored experience affects how each new communication is understood.

✧ People who are close to children can trust their instincts to know when their children need reassurance and help from them, and they can also trust that their children have ways to let them know when they've heard enough.

✧ I have always called talking about feelings "important talk." Knowing that our feelings are natural and normal for all of us can make it easier for us to share them with one another.

✧ Honesty is closely associated with freedom.

✧ In times of stress, the best thing we can do for our children (and for each other) is to listen with our ears and our hearts and to be assured that our questions are just as important as our answers.

✦ People have said "Don't cry" to other people for years and years, and all it has ever meant is "I'm too uncomfortable when you show your feelings: don't cry." I'd rather have them say, "Go ahead and cry. I'm here to be with you."

✦ If we've done our best to trust our children with the truth from the beginning, it's likely that we'll find them doing their best to trust us with it, too.

✦ Parents certainly can feel proud of themselves when they find ways to allow their children to express their real feelings and care enough to listen and talk to them.

✦ Being supportive often means waiting and listening and more waiting until you're better able to understand the drama that a certain child is living through at the moment.

✦ Fortunate parents have the freedom truth can bring them when they can trust their children enough to talk honestly with them about important and difficult things.

✧ On television I dare to say what I say and do what I do because I *know* that *somehow* those words and deeds will be translated into what's needed for whoever hears and sees. Love and trust in the space between what's said and what's heard in our life can make all the difference in this world.

✧ Laughing with someone else, of course, is the best kind of laughter. The difference between laughing *at* and laughing *with* is something children often need their parents' help in understanding. Times when families laugh together are among the most precious times a family can have.

✧ When you combine your own intuition with a sensitivity to other people's feelings and moods, you may be close to the origins of valuable human attributes such as generosity, altruism, compassion, sympathy, and empathy.

✧ I feel I've been greatly blessed by many people I've been able to meet and come to know. Sure, I've worked hard. You don't choose a job in communications and expect not to work hard. But you can expect that you don't have to do it alone. Nobody should have to do it alone. To me that's what communication is all about . . . communing in a community where people listen to themselves and others, where they try to understand what they're heard and then respond with all the creativity and care that their life has allowed them to develop.

✧ In children's play, and in all they see and do, they'll find ways to express what's on their mind. Parents do know about their children's lives, and when they listen carefully, they can find plenty of opportunities for important talk.

✧ Making up music was my most frequent way of dealing with all kinds of feelings when I was a little boy. Notes on the piano were a lot easier to disguise than words. Now I use a combination of music *and* words to communicate many of the feelings I thought I had to disguise years ago.

✧ A child's tantrum in a crowded place has pushed many a parent beyond his or her limits of self-control to the point where both parent and child lose their temper. In fact, it's hard to imagine a family where seriously angry flare-ups don't happen from time to time. Even these situations, though, can have positive outcomes. Once the incident has passed, a parent might say, for instance, "We were really angry with each other, weren't we?" That may seem like a small thing to say, but the saying of it can be a way of helping a child understand that anger is a natural and permissible human emotion; that it can be expressed and talked about; and that even when people who love each other get mad at each other, love does not diminish but sometimes even strengthens as the good feeling of harmony returns.

✧ I'd like to be able to let children know that they are not alone with their feelings—that there are other people and other children who have those kinds of feelings . . . the same fears and the same joys—to let them know there is an adult who cares.

CHAPTER NINE

Parenthood

I'm taking care of you,
Taking good care of you,
For once I was very little too.
Now I take care of you.

—FROM THE SONG
"I'M TAKING CARE OF YOU"

❧ There are no perfect parents . . . just as there are no perfect children.

❧ I don't believe children can develop in a healthy way unless they feel that they have value apart from anything they own or any skill that they learn. They need to feel they enhance the life of someone else, that they are needed. Who, better than parents, can let them know that?

❧ While some challenges our children face may make us anxious, they also present us with one of the great opportunities of parenting—the chance to resolve lingering childhood anxieties of our own. That's why I often say, "Children offer us another chance to grow."

❧ As parents, we need to try to find the security within ourselves to accept the fact that children and parents won't always like each other's actions, that there will be times when parents and children won't be able to be friends, and that there will be times of real anger in families. But we need to know, at the same time, that moments of conflict have nothing to do with whether parents and children really love one another. It's our continuing love for our children that makes us want them to become all they can be, capable of making sound choices.

❧ Being a parent is a complex thing. It involves not only trying to feel what our children are feeling and trying to know just how much to do to help them with what they cannot yet do for themselves, but also trying to know how much *not* to do. We must also learn to recognize our children's real capacities and respect their need to do things for themselves.

❧ It isn't surprising that bedtime so often brings problems in family life. After all, it raises the issue of "separation" from loved ones, and that's an issue we will continue to wrestle with all our lives.

❧ A useful suggestion for bedtime is that there be a definite amount of time—perhaps a half hour or so—for "winding down" before bedtime.

❧ Children look to adults for confirmation . . . for cues about life.

❧ One of the greatest dignities of humankind is that each successive generation is invested in the welfare of each new generation.

❧ It's not possible to be a parent without having times of worry.

✧ The major steps in growth and development don't, of course, occur in a neat and tidy sequence or at predictable intervals. What parents are most likely to notice are signs of unreadiness for certain kinds of sociability. Those signs—tantrums, fights, or a chant of "too much pee-pul"—don't have to mean a child is antisocial. What they're most likely to be are a child's way of saying, "What I need instead of a lot of someone elses right now is more time to get to know me."

✧ When fears are present, many parents try to be reassuring, telling their children not to be afraid. But for inexplicable reasons, a child may actually need to be afraid. It may be more helpful to say, "There aren't any real tigers out there, but I understand you're scared, and I'll be here to keep you safe." With reassurance like that, a child may feel strong enough to think about the "tiger" and eventually tame it.

✧ "Letting our children go" is a lifelong process for parents, one that we wrestle with again and again, and each parent has to wrestle with it in his or her own way.

✧ I know it can be frustrating for parents not to find firm answers and clear explanations for their questions and concerns, but the diversity of human beings and the uniqueness of each one strongly suggest that growth and development are not predictable.

✧ Babies who are well cared for may find in feeding time the roots of comfort and pleasure, hope and optimism, trust and whatever other ingredients go into the feeling we call love.

✧ Nighttime is an event in children's lives, and it may help to realize that—and prepare for it. A time of calmness, assurance, and closeness can be really important. For many children, the safest and most comforting place in the world is a loving lap; the most settling sound, the sound of a beloved voice.

✧ The cutting of the umbilical cord is life's first big separation for the new individual. It's a tremendously important separation for the mother, too. The ending of the actual physical attachment between the mother and the baby is the beginning of an increased emotional closeness as care and feeding begin. It's an attachment that, though invisible, is as strong and real as the umbilical cord itself.

❖ Almost all of us who have been parents have had the feeling of wanting to give our children perfect lives, lives without pain or sorrow, but of course none of us can.

❖ We want to raise our children so that they can take a sense of pleasure in both their own heritage and the diversity of others.

❖ Professional help at times when we find ourselves alarmed at our children's behavior can be helpful for children and reassuring for adults. Most of the time, though, parents cope alone, and they usually find, to their relief, that these fear-filled stages pass as mysteriously as they arrived.

❖ When should a parent worry? When should a parent ask for outside advice or help? I believe the answers are that it's all right to worry whenever you do feel worried—that the one kind of worrying parents can try to avoid is worrying about worrying itself. And the same goes for seeking advice and help: Go after it whenever you feel the need. If the first answer you get is "Don't worry, it's just a phase," then an appropriate response might be something like "Well, I am worried, and I need to know more about that phase. Where can I go to find out?" Parents who accept their worrying and use it to find the help they need often end up learning more about how children grow. What a positive outcome that can be!

✧ Long before children wonder about the mysteries of reproduction, they naturally want to know why boys and girls are made differently and what those different parts are called. For most families, that's likely to be where "sex education" begins. That time may be the most important time of all, because the way we respond to our children then can set the tone for all our later conversations about sexuality. Our earliest responses may even determine whether or not there *are* any further conversations about sex.

✧ Parents can set the example by just being themselves rather than by trying to be perfect parents. As a parent, I found it most helpful to remember the larger picture: that I really did love our sons. But there were times when I couldn't be with them. Or when I couldn't give them undivided attention. I've realized that everything does not have to be perfect in order to be effective.

✧ If we expect our children to always grow smoothly and steadily and happily, then we're going to worry a lot more than if we are comfortable with the fact that human growth is full of slides backward as well as leaps forward and is sure to include times of withdrawal, opposition, and anger, just as it encompasses tears as well as laughter.

✧ Living with a two-year-old can be a lot like living with a teen-ager, because the old, important issue of identity comes up again in the teenage years.

✧ Although we tend to think of "hello" and "good-bye" as opposites, children may treat both as aspects of the same experience: being left behind by a loved one. While parents may find themselves surprised and even hurt by their children's standoffishness at the end of a day of being apart, parents can take comfort in the thought that all it probably means is that they are loved, and loved a lot.

✧ What a wonderful thing it is to see children dealing with their own inner struggles in their own creative ways!

✧ Firstborns challenge us to grow in ways we never imagined—sometimes through their joys and sometimes through their sad and angry times. All of our children are richer when we let them know that we, too, are open to growing, even now as parents, and that we hope to go on growing all our lives long.

✧ Whenever we're anxious or uncomfortable about something our children want to do, we need to be honest with ourselves and with them and say so.

❧ I believe that infants and babies whose mothers and fathers give them loving comfort whenever and however they can are truly the fortunate ones. I think they're more likely to find life's times of trouble manageable, and I think they may also turn out to be the adults most able to pass loving concern along to the generations that follow after them.

❧ There are many ways to celebrate birthdays, and what works best for each family is what their celebration should be. After all, the reason for birthdays is to give our children a once-a-year, strong, and special confirmation of the importance of their place in our family and among their friends.

❧ It was a father who said to me, "You don't have to be a psychologist to know that young girls act differently around their fathers than around their mothers."

❧ Whatever we do to show our children we love them, nothing can replace times when we give them our complete attention. I believe that the children who have learned that there will be such times for them are the ones who are least likely to demand it and to compete for it.

✤ Each of our life journeys is unique. No child will take the same journey as the parent, and no parent can determine what a child's journey will be. Although that's a truism, we all know parents who desperately want one or more of their children to "follow in their footsteps" or "continue the family tradition."

✤ When a child first asks where babies come from, the chances are that all he or she needs is a very simple answer. A father, for instance, might reply, "Babies grow inside their mothers." It can also be a good idea to find out what answers our children have already imagined for themselves by asking, "Where do you think you came from?" Gently bringing their fantasies more in line with reality may be all we need to do . . . for a while. As they become comfortable with whatever new information we've given them, they'll let us know they're ready for more by asking again.

✤ When a person becomes a parent, he or she will not only live through the experiences of their new child but relive many of the experiences of the old child he or she once was. Such reliving is an inseparable part of "parenting."

✤ Parents are like shuttles on a loom. They join the threads of the past with the threads of the future and leave their own bright patterns as they go, providing continuity to succeeding ages.

❖ It is one of the paradoxes of parenting, and often a painful paradox, that even as our children need us for love and trust, they also need us for honest differing. It's not only differing over limits and rules. It may be differing about some of what we represent in the way of culture, traditions, and values.

❖ Parents often fear that children will be terribly disappointed when they learn that their fantasies, like the tooth fairy, are just that—fantasies. I don't believe that the disappointment is likely to be a very serious one. And when children learn the truth about who made a special wish come true, or who gave them a special gift, they learn something much more important than just "the facts."

❖ Transitions are almost always signs of growth, but they can bring feelings of loss. To get somewhere new, we may have to leave somewhere else behind. As children move out into the world (with the help of teddy bears and trust), their parents can find themselves with mixed feelings.

❖ What about when parents find themselves at the end of their ability to cope? First, I'd urge them to go on believing that problems do have causes. I'd help them know it's understandable that they're wrestling with thoughts of being "bad parents" and somehow feel that they're the cause of the trouble. But I'd like to believe that mothers and fathers in such dilemmas could remind one another during the hard times that in the persistence of their caring, they are showing one of the finest qualities of parents.

❖ No matter how often a mother picks up her child, there will be many times when she can't, times when she needs her two hands for other tasks. Her voice from the kitchen may have to make do, and her son or daughter will come to learn that full and immediate comfort isn't always available. Little by little he or she will learn to find comfort in Mother's voice instead of her arms and even discover ways to comfort him- or herself.

❖ Erik Erikson, the great authority on child development, once said, "Tradition is to human beings what instinct is to animals." Imagine what would happen if animals lost their instincts! So you can imagine how our traditions need to be considered with respect.

❖ For all parents, the birth of a child means that life will never be the same again, and each new child forces changes and reorderings of old relationships. Our pleasures and pains are now bound up in yet another's life, another's needs, experiences, feelings, triumphs, and misfortunes, and bound more closely than they may ever have been before.

❧ Somewhere built in all of us is the powerful longing for a perfect new generation. Maybe since *we're* not perfect, we could at least create someone that would be.

❧ Being a parent and a child at the same time can be very hard. It may mean feeling caught between two different sets of responsibilities and affections. As we try to sort them out, we often have an inner wrestling match between the self we were and the self we have become.

❧ Each generation, in its turn, is a link between all that has gone before and all that comes after. That is true genetically, and it is equally true in the transmission of identity. Our parents gave us what they were able to give, and we took what we could of it and made it part of ourselves. We, in turn, will offer what we can of ourselves to our children and their offspring, and they will receive what they can of it.

❧ Accepting a child's helpful participation in the life of the family is the greatest gift a grownup can offer someone who is longing to be received "exactly as I am."

❖ When a baby starts teething, both he and his parents will find themselves up against the limits of comfort: Not even holding or being held will make the pain go away. For the baby, it may be one of his earliest lessons that life will have times like that. For his parents, it will be another chance to become more comfortable with the difficult truth that there are real limits to how much comfort we can bring to loved ones when they hurt.

❖ It can be very hard to trust our own judgments as parents when our feelings seem to be different from most other people's. The best kind of friends are those who remind us that we are the ones who know most about ourselves, about our children, and about our relationships with our children.

❖ We have all been children and have had children's feelings . . . but many of us have forgotten. We've forgotten what it's like not to be able to reach the light switch. We've forgotten a lot of the monsters that seemed to live in our room at night. Nevertheless, those memories are still there, somewhere inside us.

❖ It may be painful for us to see our children modifying or even rejecting ideas that were important to us and adopting others that could never be comfortable for us. But out of that difference may come the reinforcement of two other important values. One is tolerance, and the other is awareness that people who disagree over the things they hold dear really can live together in love and respect.

❖ The people who first feed us, hold us, play with us, and talk with us help us to begin to understand who we are and who we may become. A child's very birth cries out for acceptance and care. Without these early on, he cannot survive.

❖ Parents are often puzzled because they're not aware of any circumstance that might have given rise to their children's new anxieties. While it's certainly natural to look for outside causes for such behavior, it's also easy for us to overlook changes that are oc-curring inside our children as they grow. For example, new aware-ness of their bodies and how they work often bring children new fears of anything that might intrude upon, or interfere with, the wholeness of their bodies. They can become very protective of them-selves and their privacy. A doctor's routine examination could seem quite different from one time to another if your inside feelings about yourself had changed.

✧ There's mystery in raising children: As our children grow and develop their unique talents, we can't control every aspect of their lives. For example, we can offer children music lessons and do all we can to encourage them to appreciate music, but if making music isn't their way of expressing themselves, we have to trust they'll find their own ways.

✧ Parents are extra-vulnerable to new tremors from old earthquakes. For instance, when we leave our children in child care or in preschool for the first time, it won't be just our child's feelings about being separated from us that we will have to cope with, but our own feelings as well—from our present and our past, from when we were children and struggling with our own feelings of being away from loved ones.

✧ Children's curiosity always needs to be encouraged and supported. More important than what we say is letting our children know that we welcome their asking us about anything they don't understand.

❖ In the giving of help, a parent experiences one of the best feelings that any of us can have: that life has meaning because we are needed by someone else. Watching a baby grow with our help tells us other things we like to feel about ourselves: that we are competent and loving.

❖ Parenthood is an inner change. We ourselves grow because parenting is so deep and intense.

❖ No matter how beautiful the baby is, there are always deviations from what his or her parents anticipated, and the greater those deviations, the more those parents need to have the opportunity to mourn the loss of the image of the perfect child they dreamed they would have. They need to give up the image of having the perfect child before they can appreciate the child they really do have.

❖ If the day ever came when we were able to accept ourselves and our children exactly as we and they are, then, I believe, we would have come very close to an ultimate understanding of what "good" parenting means. It's part of being human to fall short of that total acceptance—and often far short. But one of the most important gifts a parent can give a child is the gift of that child's uniqueness.

CHAPTER TEN

The Partnership Between Parents, Child-Care Providers, and Teachers

I need you
So I can be who I am . . .

A bird needs air for its wings to fly.
A boat needs water to float.
A teacher needs students who want to
         know why
An election needs a vote,
Or a lining needs a coat.

Just as I need you so I can be who I am,
You need me so you can be yourself.
We both need each other, so we can be who
         we are . . .
    —FROM THE SONG "I NEED YOU"

❖ Anything child-care providers or preschool teachers can do to preserve the essential bond between parent and child during the preschool years will help preserve the emotional health of our country.

❖ Those of us who have chosen to work with children *need* children to confirm our identities. In one way or another, we need children in order for us to be who we are. It's only natural, then, for us to feel very uncomfortable when children say they're mad at us. But it may be their only way of being in control of something.

❖ Many mothers feel severely pressured these days. They often feel like they're falling short in one part, if not several parts, of their lives. They often feel like they're failures. Well, people aren't failures when they're doing the best they can. Our performance doesn't have to be measured against anyone else's—just against our own abilities to cope.

❖ In the partnership between parent and child-care provider, both partners need to understand that there may be mixed feelings in the relationship—love and the need to be loved, guilt, anger, competition, trust, and mistrust. The more these feelings can be talked about, the more manageable they can become, and of course, the healthier the partnership will be.

✧ Do you ever wonder if you've made a difference in this life? Whether any of those children who have come to your care have remembered anything you did for them—any ways you cared for them? I believe that by the time a child grows up, that child's first teacher and second teacher and all the child's important adults will have become incorporated into that child's development. That's the way it is with all children and, although they might not remember clearly, those of us who were the educators of their early lives will always be a part of who they are. Just like those who meant so much to us when we were children will always be part of who we are.

✧ In my early training in child development, I often brought the puppets to the children. One four-year-old boy would intervene and actually prevent my being able to do much work. I remember how angry that made me. I was angry because of the frustration of my work; but I was angry at another level because when I was a little boy I wasn't allowed to prevent adults' activities like that. It took quite a while to resolve that situation, and I came to realize that one of the most important aspects of working with children is developing the capacity to differentiate between the inner child of our own past and the child we're working with in the present.

✧ The bond between baby or toddler and its mother is potentially very strong. It can stand a great deal of competition. Some mothers have experienced pangs of jealousy when their children form close relationships with another caregiver, such as a childcare provider. Research has shown, though, that no matter how attached a young child may become to the other caregiver, this remains a different kind of attachment than the one the child feels to "Mother."

✧ Whatever the options for child care are, there are two choices I would find very difficult to accept. One would be where my baby was looked after by a lot of different people, and the other would be a setting where a single person looked after many different babies. I believe that fragmented care in the early years can lead to a fragmented personality later on. It is through a strong relationship with one main caregiver in infancy and toddlerhood that a child can best develop a strong sense of self and later become capable of forming healthy relationships with others.

✧ As we work with children, what we say and do is received by each child in the light of what that child's life circumstances (and his or her reaction to those life circumstances) are at any given time.

⭐ If I was looking for a child-care provider, I'd start with a short tryout. Then I'd listen to what he or she could tell me about my child. Does the account of their time together suggest alertness, interest, and those all-important three Cs: caring, confidence, and common sense?

⭐ On the few occasions when I did something with a child's block building that was more than I was asked to do, I quickly discovered how important it was to respect the architect within the child.

⭐ Teilhard de Chardin wrote that someone scrawled the following words on the bulletin board of that great Notre Dame Cathedral: *"Le monde demain appartiendra à ceux qui lui ont apporté la plus grande espérance."* (The world tomorrow will belong to those who brought it the greatest hope.)

⭐ I believe there's no time in life when stability is more important than it is in early infancy. That's because there's no time, either, when the world is so new, so unfamiliar, seeming to change so constantly, and no time when we as infants have so little experience to bring to its understanding. Fortunate infants find the stability they need in the constancy of a face, the face of a constant caregiver.

✧ After a particularly difficult session with a child, in which I thought that I talked too much and wasn't responsive to that child, one of my supervisors said to me: "Fred, an hour with a child in which you've tried to be who you are in relationship to that child is an hour that's never wasted." And sure enough, later on in our relationship, that hour didn't turn out to be so bad.

✧ I believe that adults' successful work with children is based on our having been children ourselves and having felt good enough in those early years so that we came to believe that childhood was a time of real value. If we were loved and valued ourselves in our own childhood, we then have the opportunity to love and value the childhoods of others.

✧ When I first started working with children at a family and child-care center, as time went on, I spent hours and hours observing and listening, and little by little, something wonderful began to happen: I remembered how it felt to be a child myself. I remembered the bewilderments, the sadnesses, the joys, the lonely times, the angers. Having remembered these things, I found that I could make myself more available to the children I was with. I could take the time to listen to these children's needs before deciding what their needs were.

FRED ROGERS

❧ A teacher told me of a time when there were hurricane warnings in her area and the young children in her care seemed to want to know all about what hurricanes were. So she found out as much as she could and put what she learned in terms they could understand. But the more she told them, the more their curiosity—and anxiety—grew. One day she mentioned that if ever a hurricane happened while they were at school, she would be right there with them to help keep them safe until they could get to their parents. Then she told them that if ever there was a hurricane in their town, there were grownups who knew how to take care of children so that they wouldn't get hurt. That, it turned out, was what the children really wanted to know, and as she assured them about their safety, their fearfulness and intense curiosity subsided.

❧ In knowing who you are and being willing to share your honest self with the children in your life, you're participating in "child care."

❧ We can talk to our children about some major growth task we'd like them to do, like learning to walk or using the potty or using a cup instead of a bottle. We can find books to read together about those tasks and about the feelings that go along with trying to master them. Perhaps most important of all, we can be supportive of our children's *play* about those tasks. It's realistic for caregivers to expect to decide the time is right to suggest doing something or to encourage doing something . . . but it's probably unrealistic to decide that the day has come for a child to actually do it. That's a decision for each child to make in his or her own good time.

❖ For a child to be able to play, he or she needs the encouragement and support of another person who accepts the play in a nonjudgmental way, helping the child generate enough energy to continue the play, an available person who knows how important it is that children be able to control their play.

❖ By living and working with children, I've learned more about the child I was, the person who is always striving to grow within me.

❖ We need to remember that children are trying, too—trying to understand their feelings and their world, trying to please the people they love, trying to grow. When grownups and children are trying together, just about anything can be possible.

❧ In my years of working with the Arsenal Family and Children's Center of the University of Pittsburgh, I think of many times in my early days in which a child did something that evoked a reaction in me that really surprised me. One young boy seemed to make me continually be angry with him. Those times I felt as though I were acting like someone else. As I thought more about it, I realized that the child with whom I was working was doing his or her best to get me to act that way. The more I found out about the child's family—and particularly the father—the more I understood the fact that young children transfer their feelings about their primary caretakers onto their teachers. And what's more, that child will be very skilled in evoking behavior from adults that's like the behavior of the mother and father.

❧ For child care to be a healthy part of a child's growth, parents and child-care providers have to work together closely. The most important thing it means is that both parents and providers work together as partners to keep the child-parent relationship as strong as it can possibly be.

❧ One thing adults who work with children can do is try to understand the *meaning* of children's play in order to respond in the most helpful ways.

❖ Those of us who work with young children have a tremendous challenge. These children are going to grow up in a world that has problems we never even dreamed of.

❖ If you're a mother working outside the home who is managing to cover most of the important bases most of the time, then I think you have reason to feel good about who you are and what you are doing.

❖ Strengthen a parent . . . and you strengthen a child.

CHAPTER ELEVEN

Growing
in Adulthood

In the long, long trip of growing,
There are stops along the way
For thoughts of all the soft things
And a look at yesterday,
For a chance to fill our feelings,
With comfort and with ease,
And then tell the new tomorrow:
"You can come now when you please."

—FROM THE SONG
  "PLEASE DON'T THINK IT'S FUNNY"

❖ In the long, long trip of growing . . . there are stops along the way. It's an important moment when we need to stop, reflect, and receive. In our competitive world, that might be called a waste of time. I've learned that those times can be the preamble to periods of enormous growth. Recently, I declared a day to be alone with myself. I took a long drive and played a tape. When I got to the mountains, I read and prayed and listened and slept. In fact, I can't remember having a calmer sleep in a long, long time. The next day I went back to work and did more than I usually get done in three days.

❖ Discovering the truth about ourselves is the work of a lifetime, but it's worth the effort.

❖ Isn't it amazing how much we bring of who we've been to whatever we do today?

❖ There's an old Italian proverb: *Chi andapiano, anda sano, anda lontano.* That means: The person who goes quietly goes with health and goes far. Hurrying up and using a lot of shortcuts doesn't get us very far at all.

✧ You rarely have time for everything you want in this life, so you need to make choices. And hopefully your choices can come from a deep sense of who you are.

✧ The great poet Rilke wrote: "Be patient towards all that is unsolved in your heart, and learn to love the questions themselves."

✧ When we can resign ourselves to the wishes that will never come true, there can be enormous energies available within us for whatever we *can* do. I know a woman who remembers the time when her wish to be married and have children would not be realized. She remembers the struggle of the final resignation, and then she remembers the outcome of that resignation. Enormous energies were available to her, which she used in developing uniquely creative work with young parents.

✧ John Amos Comenius, the seventeenth-century Czech theologian, said, "Development comes from within. Nature does not hurry but advances slowly."

✧ It's true that we take a great deal of our own upbringing into our adult lives and our lives as parents; but it's true, too, that we can change some of the things that we would like to change. It can be hard, but it can be done.

✧ What makes the difference between wishing and realizing our wishes? Lots of things, and it may take months or years for a wish to come true, but it's far more likely to happen when you care so much about a wish that you'll do all you can to make it happen.

✧ Solitude is different from loneliness, and it doesn't have to be a lonely kind of thing.

✧ When I think of solitude, I think of an anecdote from *With the Door Open: My Experience* by the late Danish religious philosopher Johannes Anker-Larsen: "The most comprehensive formula for human culture which I know was given by the old peasant who, on his deathbed, obtained from his son this one promise: to sit every day for half an hour *alone* in the best room."

✧ It isn't only famous movie stars who want to be alone, and whenever I heard one speak of privacy, I find myself thinking once again how real and deep the need for such times is for all human beings . . . at all ages.

✧ It's children who have no one to trust with their feelings who may start clowning early and grow into adults who go on clowning all life long.

✧ Children who have learned to be comfortably dependent can become not only comfortably independent but also comfortable with having people depend on them. They can lean, stand, and be leaned upon, because they know what a good feeling it can be to feel needed.

✧ It came to me ever so slowly that the best way to know the truth was to begin trusting what my inner truth was . . . and trying to share it—not right away—only after I had worked hard at trying to understand it.

✧ Often out of periods of losing come the greatest strivings toward a new winning streak.

❖ All our lives, we rework the things from our childhood, like feeling good about ourselves, managing our angry feelings, being able to say good-bye to people we love . . .

❖ There's the good guy and the bad guy in all of us, but knowing that doesn't need ever to overwhelm us. Whatever we adults can do to help ourselves—and anybody else—discover that that's true can really make a difference in this life.

❖ Almost anything that extends our children's control over the world around them is bound to have a strong lure for them. In itself, that urge is a tremendous motivation for creativity and invention, for learning how to control disease or for finding ways to make deserts bloom.

❖ Some days, "doing the best we can" may still fall short of what we would like to be able to do, but life isn't perfect—on any front—and doing what we can with what we have is the most we should expect of ourselves or anyone else.

❖ The real issue in life is not how many blessings we have, but what we do with our blessings. Some people have many blessings and hoard them. Some have few and give everything away.

✧ There is no normal life that is free of pain. It's the very wrestling with our problems that can be the impetus for our growth.

✧ I recently learned that in an average lifetime a person walks about sixty-five thousand miles. That's two and a half times around the world. I wonder where your steps will take you. I wonder how you'll use the rest of the miles you're given.

✧ In the external scheme of things, shining moments are as brief as the twinkling of an eye, yet such twinklings are what eternity is made of—moments when we human beings can say, "I love you" . . . "I'm proud of you" . . . "I forgive you" . . . "I'm grateful for you" . . . "Whether you win anything or not, you still have great value." That's what eternity is made of: invisible, imperishable *good stuff*.

✧ Everyone wants to feel that he or she has something to offer. The most depressing feeling in the world is the feeling of having nothing to offer—nothing that's acceptable.

✧ It's not the honors and the prizes and the fancy outsides of life which ultimately nourish our souls. It's the knowing that we can be trusted, that we never have to fear the truth, that the bedrock of our very being is good stuff. That's what makes growing humanity the most potentially glorious enterprise on earth.

✧ As work grows out of play, an attitude toward work grows with it—an attitude that may persist all through our workaday life. That attitude can have a lot to do with how we accept challenges, how we can cope with failures, and whether we can find in the jobs we do the inner fulfillment that makes working, in and of itself, worthwhile.

✧ It's good to keep in mind that whatever age we are, the choices we have seem important to us, and that the feeling we have no choices, no matter how young or old we are, can be a source of sadness and despair.

✧ The poet Kenneth Koch has said, "You aren't just the age you are, you are all the ages you ever have been."

✧ I do love being a grandfather, and I wonder if it is because my grandfather McFeely loved me so much and I had such a good time with him.

✧ Grandparents are both our past and our future. In some ways they are what has gone before, and in others they are what we will become.

✧ There are certainly no easy answers to growing older and being gracious about it, because there are going to be some days that you just don't like it when you ache. But there are going to be other days when you can receive what others give. I don't think any of us is going to be any one way all of the time.

✧ There are times all during life when we need the inner resources to keep ourselves busy and productive all by ourselves.

✧ The person I am today, the things I like to do, the choices I make, all have roots in some relationships of the past.

✧ When I think of Robert Frost's poems, like "The Road Not Taken," I feel the support of someone who is "on my side," who understands what life's choices are like, someone who says, "I've been there, and it's okay to go on."

✧ Part of the problem with "disabilities" is that the word immediately suggests an inability to see or hear or walk or do other things that many of us take for granted. But what of people who can't feel? Or can't talk about their feelings? Or can't manage their feelings in constructive ways? What of people who aren't able to form close and strong relationships? And people who cannot find fulfillment in their lives, or those who have lost hope, who live in disappointment and bitterness and find in life no joy, no love? These, it seems to me, are the truly crippling disabilities.

✧ There is no "masculine" or "feminine" when it comes to anger or sorrow, and certainly no weakness in expressing feelings that are human and common to us all.

✧ How great it is when we come to know that times of disappointment can be followed by times of fulfillment; that sorrow can be followed by joy; that guilt over falling short of our ideals can be replaced by pride in doing all that we can; and that anger can be channeled into creative achievements . . . and dreams that we can make come true!

✧ I believe it's a fact of life that what we have is less important than what we make out of what we have. The same holds true for families: It's not how many people there are in a family that counts, but rather the feelings among the people who are there.

✧ There's no "should" or "should not" when it comes to having feelings. They're part of who we are, and their origins are beyond our control. When we can believe that, we may find it easier to make constructive choices about what to do with those feelings.

✧ An important task in any human being's growth is our discovery of our own boundaries of self.

✧ Play can continue to be a valuable tool for creative problem-solving all our lives.

✧ How many times have you noticed that it's the little quiet moments in the midst of life that seem to give the rest extra-special meaning?

✧ Many people work very hard at the things they do for fun.

✧ I hope you're proud of yourself for the times you've said "yes" when all it meant was extra work for you and was seemingly helpful only to somebody else.

✧ Please think of the *children* first. If you ever have anything to do with their entertainment, their food, their toys, their custody, their child care, their health care, their education—listen to the children, learn about them, learn from them. *Think of the children first.*

✧ One of the greatest paradoxes about omnipotence is that we need to feel it early in life, and lose it early in life, in order to achieve a healthy, realistic, yet exciting, sense of potency later on.

✧ All through our lives there are resignations of wishes. As children, once we learn to walk, we must resign ourselves to not being a baby anymore.

✧ I don't know that I'll be alive when my grandsons have children, so they just may be the last Rogerses that I'm acquainted with on this earth. I know they will have lots inside them to give their children or nieces or nephews. But still, it is really fun for me to see them doing things that I know Rogerses have done for a long, long time. There is a continuity that goes through the generations. Margaret McFarland used to say, "I love being part of the beach of life—I like being one of the grains of sand." I really love being part of humanity and stepping into the stream and stepping out of it. I have lots of thoughts about what it will be like when I am gone.

✧ The child is in me still . . . and sometimes not so still.

ACKNOWLEDGMENTS

JUST AS WE ARE a reflection of all the people who have touched us as we've lived, so, too, is our work. This book certainly represents what I've learned over many years from people who have touched my life along the way. I'd like especially to acknowledge some of them.

Everyone at Family Communications, Inc. (FCI), who has worked with me for the past twenty-seven years. Our company is like a family, and each person's work and enthusiasm have brought a valuable contribution to the development of this book, just like everything else we do. Over the past fifteen years, our writings have been greatly enhanced by the wisdom, sensitivity, and editing talents of Barry Head. Dennis Ciccone, the latest member of Family Communications Inc., gave us great assistance with the development of this book. He and Hedda Sharapan, one of the earliest members of the FCI "family," who helps in everything we do, devoted hours of dedicated work collecting the quotations and organizing the manuscript.

Our editor, Mindy Werner, and the other people at Viking whose persistence and encouragement have made this particular collection possible.

Michael Jacobs, who got us started in this project.

ACKNOWLEDGMENTS

My special thanks to all of these people—my teachers, my friends, and my family: Joanne, John and Mary, Jim and Tory, Alexander and Douglas. These past forty years of producing television programs and writing for children and their families have been very, very special.